Blueprint TWO

Brian Abbs
Ingrid Freebairn

Longman

Contents

Unit 1
Grammar
Revision of tenses
Both/neither

Unit 2
Grammar
Present perfect simple
For and *since*
Vocabulary
Word puzzle

Unit 3
Grammar
Gerund (*ing*)
Communication
Agreeing and disagreeing
Vocabulary
Crossword

Unit 4
Reading
Family life and routine
Grammar
Time phrases
Expressions of frequency
Writing
Description of family life and routine

Unit 5
Reading
Descriptions of New York
Grammar
Non-defining relative clauses with *who, which, where*
Punctuation
Commas
Writing
Description of a person

Listening and speechwork 1–5
Listening
Informal and formal conversations
Oral exercises
Agreeing and disagreeing
Adverbs of frequency
Present perfect
Pronunciation
/ə/ six **o**'clock
Stress and intonation
How far is it to Bath?
Intonation of *Wh*-questions

Unit 6
Communication
Directions

Unit 7
Grammar
Have to
Vocabulary
Jobs and personal qualities

Unit 8
Communication
Offers and requests
Accepting and refusing
Writing
Letter offering an interview

Unit 9
Grammar
Conjunctions *because/so*
Writing
A note of apology with a reason

Unit 10
Reading
About Canada
Vocabulary
Geographical features
Natural environment
Grammar
Defining relative clauses with *who, which, where*
Writing
Completing a letter

Listening and speechwork 6–10
Listening
People giving directions
Oral exercises
Asking for directions
Have to (duties)
Offers of help
Pronunciation
Consonant clusters with **l** and **r**, e.g. **pl**ease, **pr**ince
Stress and intonation
Turn right at the station.
Intonation of polite offers

Unit 11
Reading
About the Channel Tunnel
Grammar
Future time clauses with *when, as soon as*
Communication
Making promises with *will, 'll, won't*

Unit 12
Grammar
Quantity pronouns
Writing
Completing a letter
Grammar
Prepositions

Unit 13
Communication
Suggestions
Grammar
Direct and indirect objects

Unit 14
Grammar
Present perfect simple with *just, already, still, yet*
Writing
Rearranging a letter

Unit 15
Grammar
Past continuous
Vocabulary
'Fire-related' words

Listening and speechwork 11–15
Listening
Opinions of someone's facial features
Three conversations: listening for gist
Oral exercises
Will/won't (promises)
Present perfect simple
Past continuous
Pronunciation
Consonant clusters with **s**, e.g. **sk**irt, **st**art, **sn**ow
The linking /r/: fa**r a**nd wide
Stress and intonation
What was he doing at home?
Intonation of short responses

Unit 16
Reading
Letter about children's eating habits
Grammar
Too much/too many and *not enough*
Vocabulary
Types of television programmes

Unit 17
Communication
Giving advice
Should and *ought to*

Unit 18
Reading
Hotel information
Grammar
(Not) allowed to/have to
Not + adjective + *enough*

Unit 19
Communication
Reminders, advice and warnings
Vocabulary
Containers
Reading
Car accident procedures

Unit 20
Reading
Biography: David Hockney
Grammar
During, while and *for*
Before/after + (*ing*)

Listening and speechwork 16–20
Listening
Consultation with a doctor
Oral exercises
Too much/too many (complaints)
Should (advice)
Ought to (criticism)
Not allowed to
Pronunciation
Aspiration after '**p**', '**t**', '**k**': **p**ain, **t**ake, **c**ost
Double consonants: par**t** time, mi**dd**ay
Stress and intonation
Never go al**one**
Intonation of neutral and excited responses

Unit 21
Grammar
may/might/going to
Reading
The weather forecast
Writing
Letter to a friend about a future visit

Unit 22
Grammar
Ask/tell somebody to do something
Vocabulary
Collocation with verbs *turn on*, *wash*, *open*

Unit 23
Grammar
Stative verb + adjective
Stative verb + *like*
Communication
Completing a conversation using *to like/to be like/would like*

Unit 24
Reading and grammar
Could/must/can't
Writing
A note about an item lost in someone's home

Unit 25
Grammar
Reported requests with *ask* and *tell*
Want somebody to do something

Listening and speechwork 21–25
Listening
Extract from a quiz show
Oral exercises
May (possible situations)
Can't and *must* (conclusions)
Want + object pronoun + infinitive (checking instructions)
Pronunciation
Diphthongs: /aɪ/ h**igh**
/ɔɪ/ b**oy** /aʊ/ h**ow**
Double affricate consonants: oran**ge j**uice
Stress and intonation
Can you <u>tell</u> him to <u>wait</u>?
Intonation of interested responses

Unit 26
Grammar
Question tags
Communication
Checking information with question tags
Punctuation
Mixed punctuation in a letter

Unit 27
Communication
Expressing surprise with question tags
Vocabulary
Dictionary definitions

Unit 28
Grammar
Defining relative clauses omitting *who/which*
Defining and non-defining *who/which*
Vocabulary
Adjectives of quality

Unit 29
Grammar
Comparison of adjectives
Communication
Comparing sports
Vocabulary
Crossword

Unit 30
Grammar
Although, however
Linking words
Reading
About a Russian singer

Listening and speechwork 26–30
Listening
Conversation about a train accident
Oral exercises
Question tags (surprise)
Superlatives (opinions)
Not as... as/Much... -er than (comparison)
Pronunciation
Diphthongs:
/ɪə/ h**ere** /eə/ th**ere**
Assimilation: eigh**t b**oys
Stress and intonation
It's <u>much</u> more ex<u>ci</u>ting than <u>that</u>.
Intonation of rising question tags

Unit 31
Reading
About a young man's career
Grammar
Used to
Vocabulary
Modern inventions

Unit 32
Grammar
So... that
Such... that
Writing
Messages of apology with reasons

Unit 33
Grammar
First conditional + future *will/won't*
Reading
About popular psychology

Unit 34
Grammar
Past perfect
Past simple/past perfect
Vocabulary
Easily confused words

Unit 35
Grammar
Present passive
Vocabulary
Word definitions
Writing
Factual description: precious stones

Listening and speechwork 31–35
Listening
Four advertisements
Oral exercises
Used to (past facts)
If + will (consequence)
Past perfect
Present passive (processes)
Pronunciation
Consonant clusters:
/θr/ **thr**ow /str/ **str**ong
Assimilation: thi**s sh**op
Stress and intonation
I <u>used</u> to <u>wash</u> them by <u>hand</u>.
Intonation with emphatic stress

Unit 36
Grammar
Reported statements

Unit 37
Reading
Character descriptions
Grammar
Modifiers

Unit 38
Grammar
Reported questions
Reading
Rearrange parts of a story

Unit 39
Reading
Completing a story with adjectives of emotion
Grammar
Prepositions after adjectives
Vocabulary
Word formation: adjective/noun
Adjectives of stronger emotional intensity

Unit 40
Grammar
Phrasal verbs
Writing
Instructions using phrasal verbs
Vocabulary
Crossword

Listening and speechwork 36–40
Listening
A reported conversation
Oral exercises
Reported questions
Reported statements
Personal qualities
Pronunciation
Assimilation:
/dʒ/ woul**d y**ou like to
/tʃ/ ge**t y**our glass
Stress and intonation
He <u>said</u> that he <u>wanted</u> to <u>go</u> to the <u>park</u>.
Shifting stress with the same intonation

Quiz

Pronunciation table

Unit 1

Flight Arrivals

GRAMMAR: revision of tenses

PASSENGER INFORMATION
- AIRLINE: BA ☐ JAL ☐ Qantas ✓ TWA ☐
- AGE: 38
- PREVIOUS VISITS: Yes ✓ No ☐
- PURPOSE OF VISIT: To live ☐ To work ✓ To study ☐ To have a holiday ☐
- LENGTH OF STAY: Days ☐ Weeks ☐ Months ☐ Years 1

PASSENGER INFORMATION
- AIRLINE: BA ✓ JAL ☐ Qantas ☐ TWA ☐
- AGE: 24
- PREVIOUS VISITS: Yes ☐ No ✓
- PURPOSE OF VISIT: To live ☐ To work ☐ To study ☐ To have a holiday ✓
- LENGTH OF STAY: Days ☐ Weeks ☐ Months 2 Years ☐

1 Use Michael's form above to complete the interviewer's questions.

INTERVIEWER: Just a few questions, please.
1 (Which airline/fly with)
Which airline did you fly with?

MICHAEL: I flew with Qantas.

INTERVIEWER: 2 (have/good flight)
....

MICHAEL: Yes, thanks. Very pleasant.

INTERVIEWER: 3 (How old)
....

MICHAEL: I'm thirty-eight.

INTERVIEWER: 4 (Britain before)
....

MICHAEL: Yes, I have.

INTERVIEWER: 5 (What/do here)
....

MICHAEL: I'm going to work.

INTERVIEWER: 6 (How long/stay)
....

MICHAEL: I'm going to stay for a year.

INTERVIEWER: Welcome to Britain!

MICHAEL: Thanks!

2 Use Elena's form above to write a similar interview with her.

INTERVIEWER: *Just a few questions, please. Which airline did you fly with?*

ELENA: ....
INTERVIEWER: ....
ELENA: ....
INTERVIEWER: ....
ELENA: ....
INTERVIEWER: ....
ELENA: ....
INTERVIEWER: ....
ELENA: ....
INTERVIEWER: ....
ELENA: ....
INTERVIEWER: ....
ELENA: ....

3 Tom and Sam work in an office together. Complete their conversation with positive and negative statements.

TOM: Are you busy, Sam?
SAM: No. It's all right.
1 (checking a letter/X do anything special)
I'm checking a letter. I'm not doing anything special

TOM: Did you see 'Dial M for Murder' last night?
SAM: No.
2 (go out last night/X watch television)
....
....

TOM: Oh, you missed a good film. I've just come back from lunch at the Pizza Corner. Have you ever been there?
SAM: 3 (the Pizza House/X the Pizza Corner)
....
....

TOM: What did you have for lunch?
SAM: 4 (some sandwiches/X a hot meal)
....
....

TOM: What are you going to do this weekend?
SAM: 5 (visit some friends in the country/X stay in town)
....
....
....

TOM: That sounds nice. I'm going to the opera on Saturday. Have you got a black tie I can borrow?
SAM: 6 (dark blue tie/X black one)
....
....

TOM: Don't worry. I'll ask Mark. See you later.

4 Complete the paragraph with the correct tense of the verb in brackets.

Harry Best (live) [1] *lives* with his wife, Elsie, in a small town near Birmingham. They (not/have got) [2] .... any children. Every day Harry (go) [3] .... to work in Birmingham on the 8.45 train and he (come) [4] .... home at five thirty every evening.

Every summer Harry and Elsie (go) [5] .... on holiday to the seaside. They always (stay) [6] .... in England because Harry (not/like) [7] .... foreign food and neither of them (speak) [8] .... any foreign languages. Last summer they (go) [9] .... to Blackpool for their holidays and (stay) [10] .... in a small hotel but next year they (rent) [11] .... a cottage on the south coast of England, near Brighton. At the moment they (look) [12] .... at holiday brochures and they (get) [13] .... quite excited. They (never/be) [14] .... to the south coast before.

GRAMMAR: both/neither

5 Look at Exercises 1 and 2 again. Complete the sentences about Michael and Elena using *both of them, one of them* or *neither of them* and the correct form of the verb where necessary.

1 *Both of them are* staying for over a month.
2 .... under forty.
3 .... going to study in Britain.
4 .... travelled by JAL.
5 .... been to Britain before.

Unit 2

GRAMMAR: present perfect simple

1 Choose a response from the box and add a question starting with *how long*.

> No, I didn't.   Yes, please!   How exciting!
> Congratulations! (x2)   That's good!
> I'm terribly sorry!   Oh dear!

1 It's our wedding anniversary today.
   (be/married) *Congratulations! How long have you been married?*

2 The television is broken unfortunately.
   (be/broken) ....

3 Do you want a ride in my new car?
   (have/it) ....

4 Did you know Jenny wore contact lenses?
   (wear/them) ....

5 Where were you? It's ten past six!
   (be/here) ....

6 Kevin and I are getting married next autumn.
   (know/him) ....

7 They live in Thailand now!
   (live/there) ....

8 The job is very easy for me now.
   (work/here) ....

2 Complete the sentences with *for* or *since*.

1 I've been here ...*since*... last Monday.
2 He's worked here .... six years.
3 We've lived here .... we got married.
4 I've known her .... ten years.
5 It hasn't rained .... last month.
6 I haven't seen her .... a long time.
7 The hotel has been open .... a year.
8 He hasn't worked .... his accident.

VOCABULARY

3 Use the clues to complete the word puzzle and find mystery word number 9.

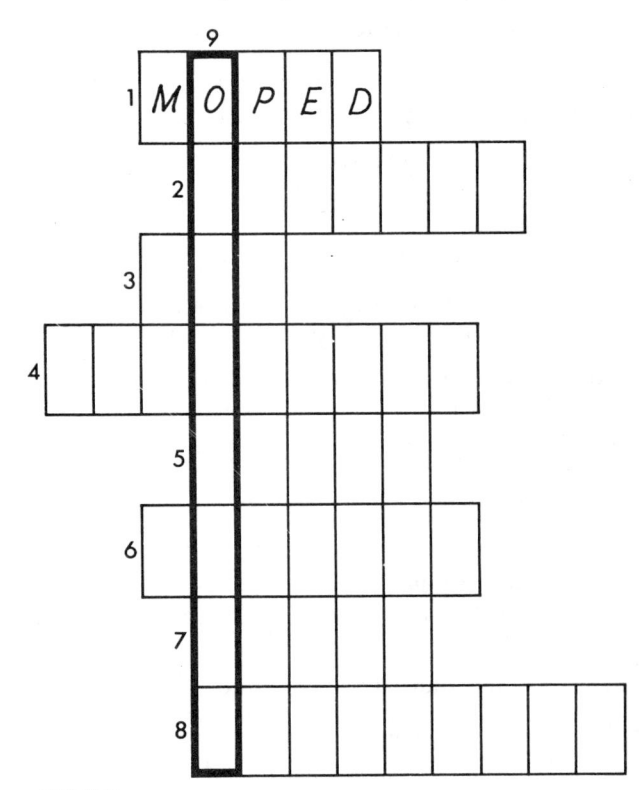

1 M O P E D

CLUES

1 Smaller than a motorbike.
2 Smaller than a town.
3 An animal which people keep at home.
4 Josh wants a job as this.
5 I've been here . . . lunchtime.
6 Opposite of *both*.
7 If you want a job you must . . . for it.
8 When you arrive in a new place you must find . . . to live.

9 ....

3

Unit 3

GRAMMAR: gerund (*ing*)

1 Use the picture prompts to talk about people's likes and dislikes.

☺ = enjoy   ☺ = not mind   ☹ = hate

1 fly ☺
2 cook ☹
3 vacuum ☺
4 wear ☹
5 camp ☺
6 clean ☹

1 John *doesn't mind flying*
2 Sue and her sister ....
3 Martin ....
4 Dave ....
5 Jill and Simon ....
6 Bobby ....

COMMUNICATION: agreeing and disagreeing

2 Agree with the statements using *So do I* or *Nor do I*.

1 I don't like American food.   *Nor do I*
2 I think gardening is boring.   ....
3 I enjoy a game of cards.   ....
4 I always plan my holidays early.   ....
5 I never wear gloves.   ....
6 I don't eat meat.   ....

3 Disagree with the statements using *I do* or *I don't*.

1 I don't like watching TV.   *I do*
2 I like getting up early.   ....
3 I never get jet lag.   ....
4 I always eat a big breakfast.   ....
5 I don't mind working late.   ....

VOCABULARY

4 Complete the crossword.

CLUES
Across
1 You do the ... ... after a meal. (7, 2)
3 ... the carpets takes a long time. (9)
5 Opposite of *dirty*. (5)
7 You go ... to buy food. (8)
9 After you wash and dry your clothes you do the ... (7)
10 A hobby for people who like plants and flowers. (9)

Down
2 People live in this. (5)
4 Boys grow up to be ... (3)
5 A chef does this in a restaurant. (7)
6 ... your bed is a daily job. (6)
7 Divide between two or more people. (5)
8 When you turn on the vacuum cleaner, it makes a lot of ... (5)

Crossword: 1 Across: WASHING UP

Unit 4

A new life for the Yeungs in Newcastle

Lee Yeung and his family came from Hong Kong to Newcastle, in the north-east of England, three years ago. Lee is a buyer for a big department store in Newcastle. He always works a very long day from 8 a.m. to 7 p.m. and he occasionally likes to go out for a drink with his English friends after work.

ENGLISH FOOD

At home Mr and Mrs Yeung eat Chinese food every day, but the children quite often eat English food. The whole family goes to a Chinese restaurant on the coast to enjoy fresh fish on Saturdays. The children like the same things as their British school friends: pop music, films and TV. They go to the cinema about once a fortnight and Mrs Yeung watches TV with her children every evening. She also goes to an English class at her daughter's school once a week on Friday afternoons. Lee usually plays golf at the weekend.

PARKS AND OPEN SPACES

Lee says he likes the parks and open spaces in England. He also likes the holidays. In Hong Kong he only got one holiday a year. In Britain he gets a holiday three times a year. Lee also likes travelling. He often drives his family to Scotland and they sometimes visit other European countries. Mrs Yeung says: 'My family like it here but it's more difficult for me. I hardly ever see my friends from Hong Kong. My future is in Britain but my past and my heart are in Hong Kong.'

The family at home in Newcastle

READING

1 Read about the Yeung family and complete the information.

The family at home in Newcastle

Family name	*Yeung*
Country of origin	
Present home town	
Length of time there	
Job	
Hours	
Holidays	
Family activities	*going to a Chinese restaurant on Saturdays*
Interests: children's	
wife's	
Lee's	*going out with friends for a drink*

GRAMMAR: time phrases

2 Answer with a time phrase.

When:

1 did the Yeungs move to England?
   Three years ago

2 does Mr Yeung start work?
   ....

3 does Mr Yeung like to go out for a drink with his English friends?
   ....

4 do the family eat at a Chinese restaurant?
   ....

5 does Mrs Yeung go to an English class?
   ....

6 does Mr Yeung play golf?
   ....

GRAMMAR: expressions of frequency

3 Answer with an adverb of frequency.

How often:
1 does Mr Yeung get home after 7 p.m.?
Always.

2 does Mr Yeung play golf at the weekend?
....

3 do the children eat English food at home?
....

4 does the family visit other European countries?
....

5 does Mr Yeung like to go out for a drink?
....

6 does Mrs Yeung see her friends from Hong Kong?
....

7 do Mr and Mrs Yeung eat English food?
....

4 Answer with an adverbial phrase of frequency.

How often:
1 do Mr and Mrs Yeung eat Chinese food?
Every day.

2 do the children watch TV?
....

3 does Mrs Yeung go to an English class?
....

4 do the children go to the cinema?
....

5 does Mr Yeung get a holiday?
....

5 Rewrite the sentences using the words in brackets.

1 The library is open on Sunday. (never)
The library is never open on Sunday.

2 They're late. (hardly ever)
....

3 She eats meat. (occasionally)
....

4 He's late for work. (every day)
....

5 I'm there on business. (often)
....

6 We go to the cinema. (once a month)
....

7 I don't agree with her. (usually).
....

8 It's raining when I want to go out. (always)
....

WRITING

6 Use the chart and the text in Exercise 1 to write in your notebook about Pierre Udry and his family. Start like this:

Pierre Udry came from Switzerland to London . . .

Name	Pierre Udry
Country of origin	Switzerland
Present home town	London
Length of time there	2 years
Job	Computer engineer
Hours	8.30 a.m.–6.30 p.m.
Holidays	twice a year
Family activities	– French restaurant on Friday evenings – swimming every Sunday afternoon – cinema occasionally

Unit 5

SPOTLIGHT ON NEW YORK

'When you say the word "Manhattan", a lot of people think of big stores, skyscrapers and hotels. They forget about Greenwich Village, which for me is the heart of the city. This area, where people go to look at art, the latest fashions, old films and bookshops, is the exact opposite to Fifth Avenue and Park Lane.'
A tourist from Amsterdam

'Unfortunately, New York is expensive. You pay for everything. My child fell off her bicycle in Central Park. An ambulance took her to the Roosevelt Hospital and I got a bill for 180 dollars. It's a tough city.'
A New Yorker

'Harlem, which is sometimes called Black Manhattan, is well-known for its street life and lively people. It is especially famous for its music and its jazz clubs. Louis "Satchmo" Armstrong and Duke Ellington, who were two of the greatest jazz musicians of our time, first started to play there.'
A New York tourist guide

READING

1 Read the comments about New York and answer the questions.

1 What do some people think of when they hear the word 'Manhattan'?
They think of big stores, skyscrapers and hotels.

2 Which area of New York does the tourist from Amsterdam prefer?
....
....

3 What can you see there?
....
....

4 What does the New Yorker say is one of the problems about living in New York?
....
....

5 How much was his hospital bill?
....
....

6 What is Harlem especially famous for?
....
....

GRAMMAR: non-defining relative clauses with *who*

2 Join two facts with a *who* clause to make a sentence.

1 *Frank Lloyd Wright, who was an architect, designed the Guggenheim Museum in New York.*

2 Ernest Hemingway, ...
....

3 George Gershwin, ...
....

4 Margaret Mead, ...
....

5 Martin Luther King, ...
....

6 Margaret Bourke-White, ...
....

1 FRANK LLOYD WRIGHT (1869–1959)
An architect. Designed the Guggenheim Museum in New York.

2 ERNEST HEMINGWAY (1898–1961)
One of America's most famous novelists. Wrote *A Farewell to Arms* and *For Whom the Bell Tolls*.

3 GEORGE GERSHWIN (1898–1937)
A composer. Wrote the music for the folk-opera *Porgy and Bess*.

4 MARGARET MEAD (1901–1978)
An anthropologist. Became famous through her studies of people in different cultures.

5 MARTIN LUTHER KING (1929–1968)
A black clergyman and civil rights leader. Won the Nobel Peace Prize in 1964.

6 MARGARET BOURKE-WHITE (1904–1971)
The first woman photo journalist. Took photographs all over the world for *Life* magazine.

GRAMMAR: non-defining relative clauses with *which* and *where*

3 You are in New York. Use the chart below to write sentences about your stay.

Name	Type	Location	When
RESTAURANTS			
Alfredo	Italian	Uptown	yesterday
Bibliotheque	French	Midtown	last Wednesday
Sam Wo	Cantonese	Downtown	next Monday
SHOPS			
Bloomingdale's	department store	Lexington Avenue	tomorrow
Unique	boutique	West Broadway	the day after tomorrow
Dean and Deluca	food store	Broadway	two days ago
CLUBS			
The Factory	Jazz	SoHo	last Saturday evening
The Bottom Line	Rock	Chelsea	yesterday
Kilimanjaro	Reggae and salsa	Queens	tomorrow

1 *Yesterday I went to Alfredo's, which is an Italian restaurant in Uptown Manhattan.*

2 ......

3 ......

4 *Tomorrow I'm going to Bloomingdale's, which is a department store on Lexington Avenue.*

5 ......

6 ......

7 *Last Saturday evening I went to a club in SoHo called The Factory, where you can listen to jazz.*

8 ......

9 ......

PUNCTUATION

4 Look at the notes about Louis Hymes and put commas in the paragraph about him.

Louis Hymes who is twenty-five is a police officer. He lives on Staten Island which is in New York. Louis lives with his mother who is a widow. When he is off duty he likes to go to Radio City where he meets his girlfriend Patti. Afterwards he takes her home on his moped to New Jersey where she is studying.

WRITING

5 In your notebook, make a list of facts about a friend or relative and then write a similar paragraph.

Listening and speechwork 1–5

A   B   C

LISTENING

1 Listen to three conversations. Match each conversation with the correct picture above and tick if the conversation is informal, formal or semi-formal.

	Picture	Informal	Formal	Semi-formal
Conversation 1	C			
Conversation 2				
Conversation 3				

2 Now listen to the conversations again. Write *Yes* or *No* for each conversation.

	Conversation 1	Conversation 2	Conversation 3
They have met before.	No		
They talk about the weather.			
They talk about the journey.			
They talk about the place.			
They talk about the food.			

ORAL EXERCISES

3 Agree with someone.

T: I quite like shopping
S: *So do I.*
T: I don't like ironing.
S: *Nor do I.*

1 shopping   4 gardening
2 ironing   5 cooking
3 washing up   6 do/housework

4 Disagree with someone.

T: I don't mind waiting.
S: *I do.*
T: I quite like horror films.
S: *I don't.*

1 waiting   4 meat
2 horror films 5 big cities
3 champagne   6 soap operas

10

5 Disagree strongly with someone.

T: *You're always late.*
S: *No, I'm not. I'm never late.*
T: *She never goes there.*
S: *Yes, she does. She always goes there.*

1 I/never
2 she/always
3 they/always
4 you/never
5 he/always
6 they/never

6 Say how long you have done things.

T: *Do you work here?*
S: *Yes, I've worked here since September.*
T: *Do you know him well?*
S: *Yes, I've known him for ten years.*

1 September
2 ten years
3 1989
4 8 o'clock
5 five years

PRONUNCIATION

> **Weak vowel sound**
> /ə/ six o'clock

7 Listen and circle the weak vowels in these phrases.

1 It's for you.
2 How's the car?
3 It's a girl.
4 Go to bed.
5 Come at three.
6 Lots of fun.

Now listen and repeat the phrases.

STRESS AND INTONATION

> **Sentence stress**
> o O o o o O
> How far is it to Bath?

8 Listen and underline the stressed words.

1 How far is it to Bath?
2 How long has he been home?
3 How often does she go?
4 How many do you want?

Now listen and repeat the questions.

> **Intonation of Wh-questions**
> Where did she go?

9 Listen to the conversation and repeat the question each time. Make your voice fall at the end of each question.

T1: *Sue went for a walk last week.*
T2: *Where did she go?*
S: *Where did she go?*

1 Where did she go?
2 How far did she walk?
3 Who did she meet?
4 Which restaurant did they go to?
5 What did they have to eat?
6 How long did they stay?
7 What was the problem?

Unit 6

COMMUNICATION: directions

1 You are at the Tourist Information Centre in Oxmouth. Look at the map and write the requests for these directions.

1 *Excuse me, can you tell me the way to the Union Hotel?*

Go along College Street, take the third turning on the right into Union Street, and it's about half way down on your left.

2 *Excuse me, can you tell me the way to the College street*

Go along College Street, turn left at the town hall into Union Street and it's on your left, past the youth hostel.

3 *Excuse me, can you tell me the way to the Library*

Walk down College Street as far as the traffic lights, turn left into Ferry Street and it's on your right.

4 ....

Walk down College Street and it's right at the other end of the street.

2 You are at the Tourist Information Centre in Oxmouth. Use the map to give directions.

1 Excuse me, can you tell me the way to the Maritime Museum?

Go along College Street, take the first turning on the right into Museum Street and the museum is on the right

2 Excuse me, can you tell me the way to the youth hostel?

Go along college street and take the next left

3 Excuse me, how do I get to Lloyds Bank?

Go along College street, take the second right

4 Excuse me, can you tell me the way to the bus station?

Go along College street to the end take the four turn right (ferry street). Bus station is on your left

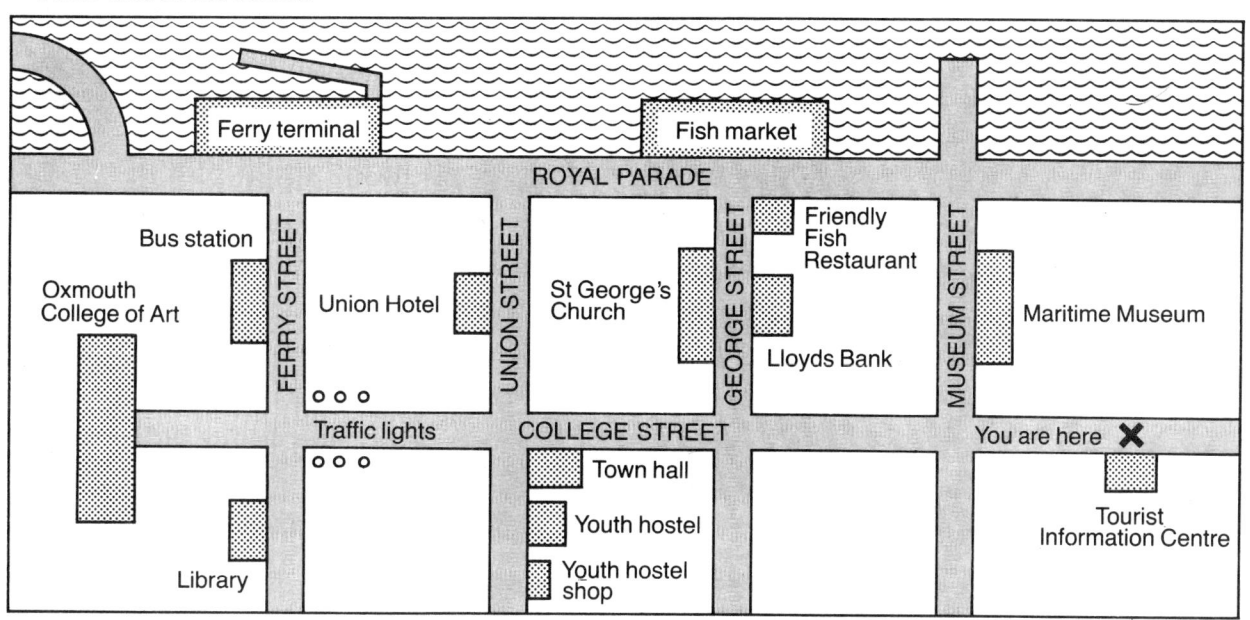

12

Unit 7

GRAMMAR: *have to*

1 Gloria Steele is a travel representative in Spain. Look at the programme and write what people have to do.

Monday	— meet new arrivals at the airport
	— guests to leave passports with Reception
Tuesday	— organise a welcome party
Wednesday	— arrange a quiz night in town
	— guests to pay for their day trip to Granada
Thursday	free
Friday	— day trip to Granada
Saturday	— go with guests to the Flamenco Dancing Show
Sunday	— guests leave the hotel at 6.30 a.m.

1 What does Gloria have to do on Mondays?
   She has to meet the new arrivals at the airport.

2 What do the guests have to do with their passports?
   She has The guest have to leave passports with reception

3 What does Gloria have to do on Tuesday?
   She has to organise a welcome party

4 What do the guests have to do on Wednesday?
   The guest have to free

5 What does Gloria have to do on Thursday?
   .... anything.

6 What do the guests have to do on Sunday?
   ....

2 Complete the dialogue with the correct form of *have to*.

MAN: I [1] *had to* go to hospital yesterday.

WOMAN: Did [2] *have to* wait long?

MAN: No, [3] *have to* wait at all.

WOMAN: That's good.

MAN: How's John?

WOMAN: He's not very well. He [4] *has to* stay off work all last week.

MAN: [5] *Have to* call a doctor?

WOMAN: Yes, and the doctor says he [6] *has to* stay at home and rest for two weeks.

VOCABULARY

3 Complete the sentences with the correct word from Unit 7.

JOBS (nouns)

A person who:

1 cuts people's hair in a salon is a *hairdresser.*

2 helps to look after people in hospital is a *n*..................

3 writes books is a *w*..................

4 designs and builds bridges is an *e*..................

5 wears and shows clothes to the public is a *m*..................

QUALITIES (adjectives)

A person who:

6 can always find a way to solve a difficult problem is *r*..................

7 doesn't mind waiting is *p*..................

8 other people can trust is *r*..................

9 manages to do things quickly and correctly is *e*..................

10 is good with his/her hands is *p*..................

Unit 8

COMMUNICATION: offers and requests

1 Complete the bubbles for each picture, using *shall, could, may* and *can*.

1 ask a question

2 help you

3 hold the baby

4 borrow your newspaper

COMMUNICATION: accepting and refusing

2 Match an offer, 1–6, with an acceptance or a refusal, a)–f).

1 Shall I clear the table?
2 Can I use your phone?
3 Could I borrow your moped?
4 May I close the window?
5 Could I look at your newspaper?
6 Shall I open that bottle for you?

a) Thank you very much.
b) I'm afraid it isn't mine.
c) Certainly. It's in the hall.
d) No, it's all right, thanks. I'll do it.
e) Yes, of course. It is a bit cold.
f) No, I'm sorry. You're not insured.

1 [d] 2 [ ] 3 [ ]
4 [ ] 5 [ ] 6 [ ]

WRITING

3 You receive the letter below. Read it and then use the information and the model to write a reply in your notebook.

> Dear . . . ,
> Thank you for your reply to our advertisement. We are interviewing candidates for this job on Monday, 28th August. I am pleased to offer you an interview at 2.30 p.m. on that date and look forward to meeting you.
>
> Yours sincerely,
>
> JButler
>
> Joanna Butler
> MANAGING DIRECTOR

Thank Ms Butler for the offer of an interview. Unfortunately you can't go because you have to attend an important meeting with your boss at 2 p.m. on 28th August. Ask if she could change the interview to the morning.

Dear . . .
Thank you for your letter asking me to . . .
Unfortunately, . . . because I . . . Could . . .
Yours sincerely,
. . .

14

Unit 9

GRAMMAR: conjunctions *because/so*

1 Choose one of the words in the box to make questions and answers using the cues.

| asleep | ill | nervous | late | bored |

1 he not/eat/dinner?
Why didn't he eat his dinner?
Because he was ill.

2 they/take/taxi?
....
....

3 he/not/pass driving test?
....
....

4 they/fall asleep?
....
....

5 she/not/answer/phone?
....
....

2 Use the questions and answers in Exercise 1 to write sentences using *so*.

1 *He was ill so he didn't eat his dinner.*

2 ....
....

3 ....
....

4 ....
....

5 ....
....

GRAMMAR: conjunctions

3 Join each pair of sentences to make a longer sentence. Use each of the conjunctions in the box twice.

| and | but | because | so |

1 She locked the door. She went to bed.
She locked the door and went to bed.

2 She was a bit nervous. She wasn't frightened.
....

3 The film was boring. I left.
....

4 I left. The class was too difficult.
....

5 The shop opens at 9 a.m. It closes at 6 p.m.
....

6 My husband was ill. I had to take the children to school.
....

7 The bus was slow. There was a lot of traffic.
....

8 I'd like to go. I can't go on Saturday.
....

WRITING

Charles,
I've got to go to the dentist at 3 o'clock on Monday so I'm afraid I'm going to be a bit late for our tennis game. I completely forgot about it. I hope that's all right.
Sorry!
Mark

4 You have promised to have coffee with your neighbours, Robert and Melanie, on Saturday at 11 a.m. In your notebook, write a note to them, saying you are going to be late and why. Use the note above to help you.

15

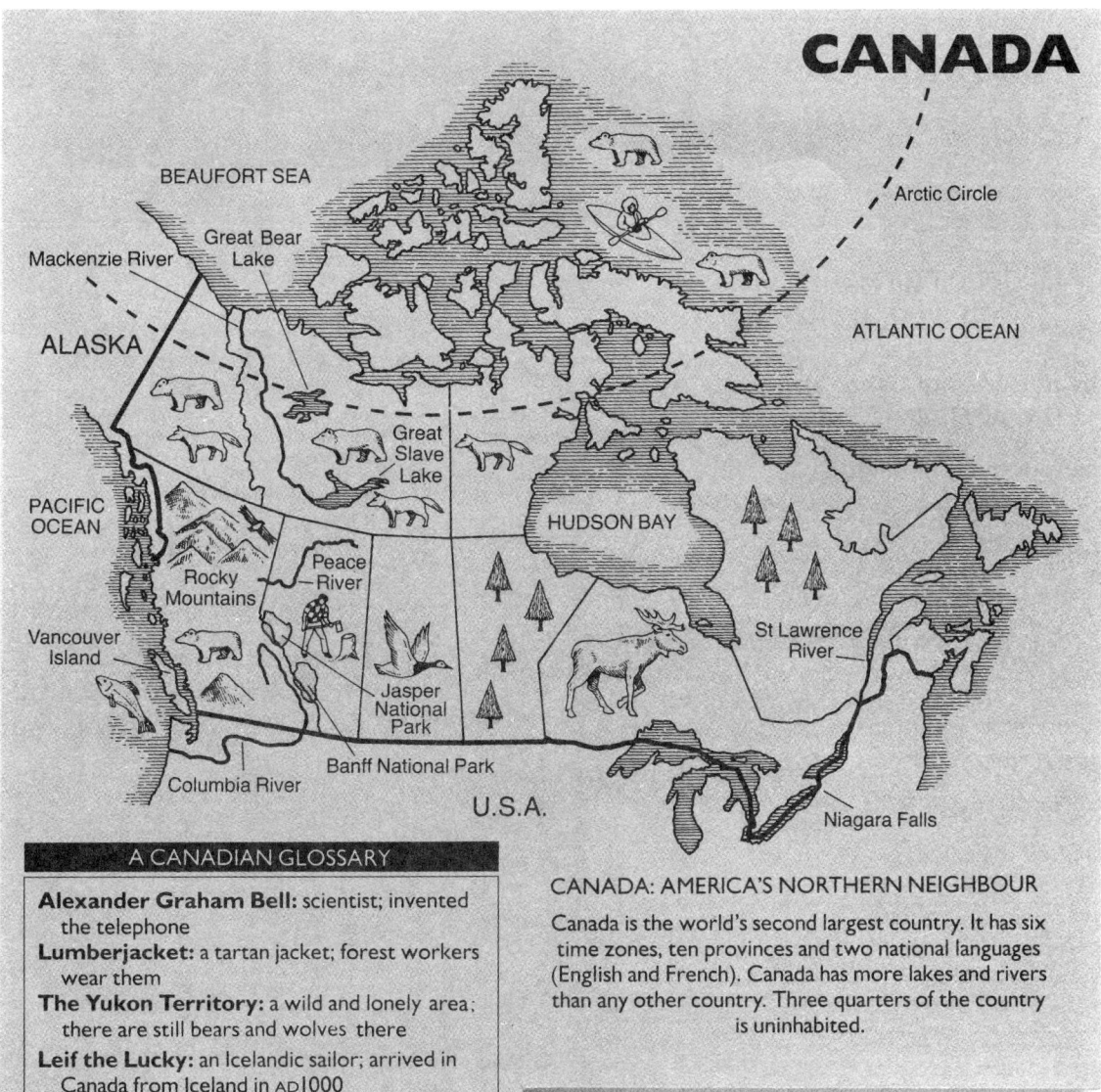

Unit 10

CANADA

A CANADIAN GLOSSARY

Alexander Graham Bell: scientist; invented the telephone
Lumberjacket: a tartan jacket; forest workers wear them
The Yukon Territory: a wild and lonely area; there are still bears and wolves there
Leif the Lucky: an Icelandic sailor; arrived in Canada from Iceland in AD1000
Niagara Falls: spectacular waterfalls on the American border; couples like to spend their honeymoon there
Snowgoose: a Canadian grey goose; flies to Scandinavia in the summer
Alexander Mackenzie: a Scottish explorer; found a way through the Rocky Mountains to the Pacific Ocean
The Rocky Mountains: high mountains in British Columbia; you can see eagles and bears in the wild

CANADA: AMERICA'S NORTHERN NEIGHBOUR

Canada is the world's second largest country. It has six time zones, ten provinces and two national languages (English and French). Canada has more lakes and rivers than any other country. Three quarters of the country is uninhabited.

VOCABULARY

1 Use the map to complete the names of these places.

1 Beaufort *Sea*
2 Hudson ....
3 Vancouver ....
4 Rocky ....
5 Pacific ....
6 Great Bear ....
7 Banff National ....
8 Niagara ....

2 Match each word in the column with a 'smaller' version of the word from the box.

| stream | bush | wood | path | sea |
| beach | stone | | | |

1 rock ....*stone*....
2 coast ....
3 tree ....
4 ocean ....
5 road ....
6 forest ....
7 river ....

GRAMMAR: defining relative clauses with *who, which, where*

3 Use the notes about Canada on page 16 to answer the questions.

1 Who was Alexander Graham Bell?
He was a scientist who invented the telephone.

2 What's a lumberjacket?
It's a tartan jacket which forest workers wear.

3 What's the Yukon Territory?
It's a wild and lonely area where there are still wolves and bears.

4 Who was Leif the Lucky?
....

5 What are Niagara Falls?
....

6 What's a snowgoose?
....

7 Who was Alexander Mackenzie?
....

8 What are the Rocky Mountains?
....

WRITING

4 Complete the letter with *who, which* or *where*.

Dear Carol,

I'm having a great time here in Canada. It really is a beautiful country. I've got a room with a family. I'm enclosing a photo of them [1]........ I took last week.

The girl [2]........ is holding the dog is the daughter, Tina. The mother is called Sarah. She's the one [3]........ is sitting on the left. Her husband, Roy, is the man in the dark jacket. The boy [4]........ is sitting on the right is their thirteen-year-old son, Dominic. Their other son, Richard, is standing between Tina and Roy. The dog is called Rufus. Have you ever met a dog [5]........ liked ice cream? This one does. The park [6]........ I took the photograph is quite near their house. It's beautiful round there!

See you soon.

Best wishes,
Sue

Listening and speechwork 6–10

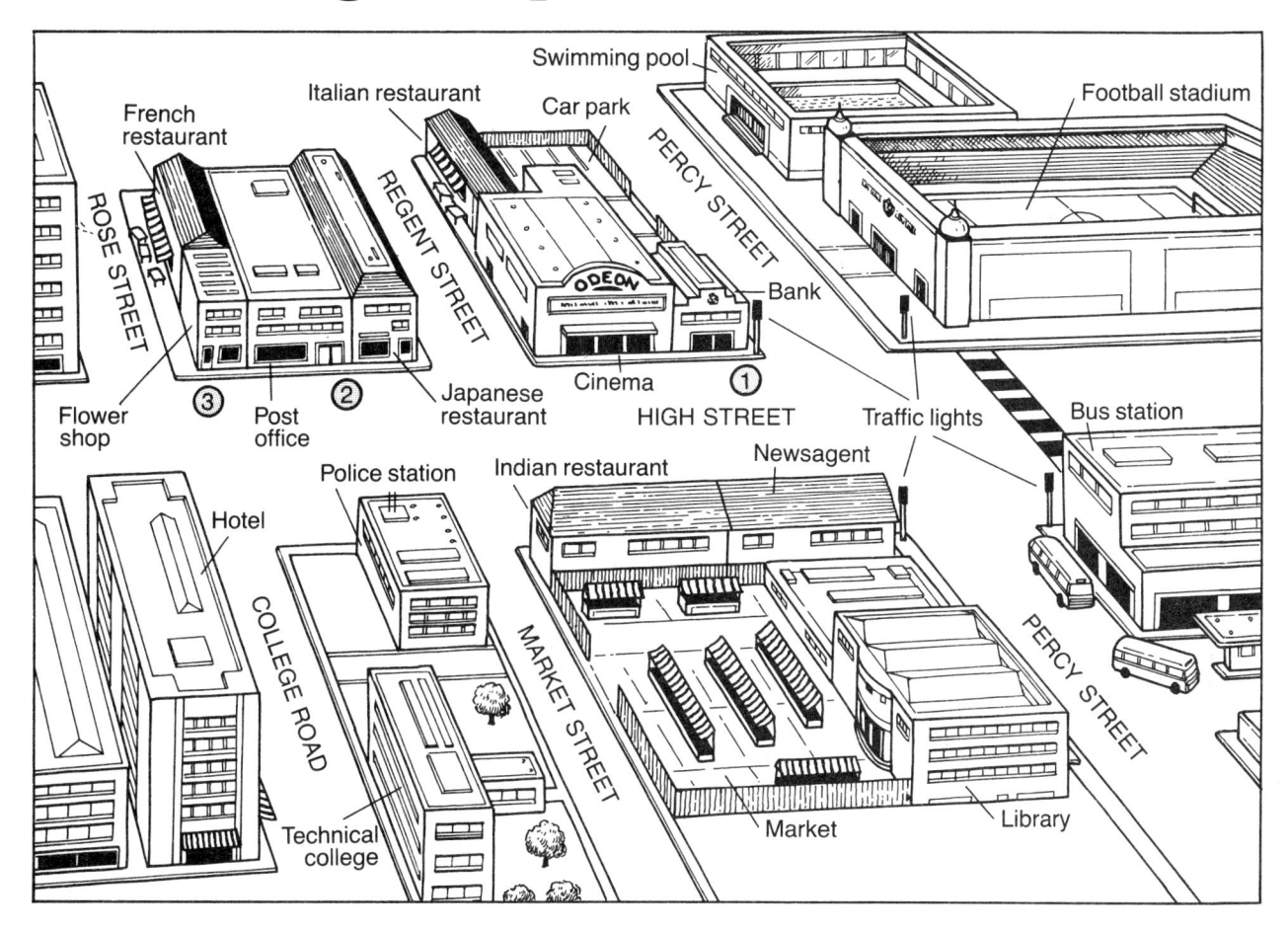

LISTENING

1 You are going to hear three conversations. Before you listen, look at the map and find where the people (1, 2 and 3) are standing in each conversation. Then listen to each conversation and note down where each person wants to go.

Conversation ① ....
Conversation ② ....
Conversation ③ ....

ORAL EXERCISES

2 Ask for directions.

T: Ask the way to the youth hostel.
S: *Excuse me. Can you tell me the way to the youth hostel, please?*

1 youth hostel
2 football stadium
3 underground station
4 sports centre
5 ticket office
6 bus station

3 Talk about duties.

T: Do we have to get up early?
S: *Yes, you have to get up at 6.30.*

1 6.30
2 before midday
3 on Monday
4 in January
5 next month
6 today

4 Offer to help.

T: Oh dear. I can't open this tin.
S: *Shall I open it for you?*

1 open
2 post
3 carry
4 find
5 get
6 answer

PRONUNCIATION

Consonant clusters with *l* and *r*
/p/b/k/g/f/ + l please
/p/b/k/g/f/ + r prince

5 Listen and tick the word you hear.

1 play ...✓... pray ....
2 crowd .... cloud ....
3 flight .... fright ....
4 glass .... grass ....
5 blue .... brew ....

6 Listen and repeat the words and phrases.

please   clean   flight   bring   great
black   glass   prince   crash   from

Please bring some clean glasses.
a great big black cloud
a Christmas present from Granny

STRESS AND INTONATION

Sentence stress
○ ○ ○ ○ ○
Turn right at the station.

7 Listen and underline the stressed syllables.

1 Turn right at the station.
2 Turn left at the theatre.
3 Turn left into Park Street.
4 Wait here at the entrance.
5 Our house is the red one.

Now listen and repeat the directions.

Intonation of polite offers
Can I help you?

8 Listen to the conversation and repeat the offers of help.

T1: Oh dear. Where am I?
T2: Can I help you?
S: *Can I help you?*

1 Can I help you?
2 Shall I take it for you?
3 Shall I get a ticket for you?
4 Shall I change it for you?

Unit 11

THE CHANNEL TUNNEL

The Channel Tunnel will provide a new fast link between Britain and France. Running under the Channel, it will consist of two passenger tunnels and one service tunnel. The tunnels will be 50 km (31 miles) long, 7.6 m (24 ft) in diameter and 34.32 km (130 ft) under the sea bed. Cars and lorries will travel on special trains leaving every three minutes. The crossing under the Channel will take thirty minutes and the total journey time from London to Paris will take three and a quarter hours, compared with the present six and a half hours.

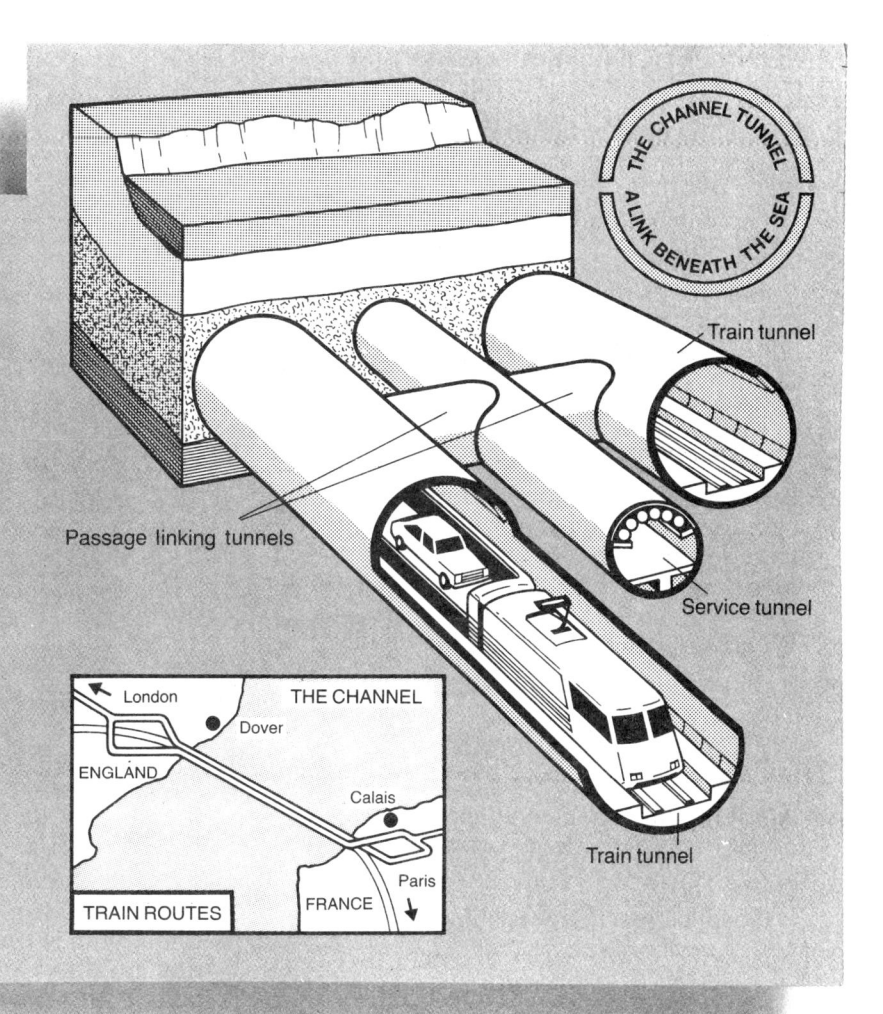

READING

1 Read about the Channel Tunnel and answer the questions.

1 How long will the tunnels be?
They will be 50 km

2 Will people be able to drive their cars across?
Yes, they will be able to drive their cars across

3 How often will the trains cross the Channel?
The trains will cross the Channel every three times

4 How long will the crossing from Dover to Calais take?
It will take thirty minutes

5 How long will the complete journey from London to Paris take?
It'll take three and a quarter hours

GRAMMAR: time clauses in the future with *when* and *as soon as*

2 Make sentences starting with *When* or *As soon as*.

1 I/get home//go straight to bed
When *I get home, I'll go straight to bed*.

2 he/arrive//he/phone you
As soon as *he arrives, he'll phone you*

3 we/decide about the job//we/let you know
As soon as *we decide about the job, we'll let you know*

4 you/see Malcolm//you/not recognise him
When *you see Malcolm, you won't recognise him*

5 I/pass my driving test//I/buy/car
As soon as *I pass my driving test, I'll buy car*

20

COMMUNICATION: making promises

3 Complete the conversation by making promises.

HELEN: Oh no. My button has come off and I've got to go.

MUM: Come on.
1 (mend it now/not take long)
I'll mend it now. It won't take long.

HELEN: Thanks, Mum.

MUM: By the way, can you buy Danny a nice cake for his birthday on your way home? Here's some money.

HELEN: O.K.

MUM: Where are you going to put the money?

HELEN: 2 (put it in my bag/not lose it)
*I'll put it in my bag.
I won't lose it.*

MUM: All right. But you mustn't tell Danny about it. It's got to be a surprise.

HELEN: Don't worry.
3 (keep it a secret/not tell him)
*I'll keep it a secret.
I won't tell him.*

MUM: What time will you be home?

HELEN: 4 (home at five/not be late)
*I'll home at five.
I won't be late.*

MUM: By the way, you must take back your library books.

HELEN: 5 (do it tomorrow/not forget)
*I'll do it tomorrow.
I won't forget.*

MUM: All right. Have a nice day.

HELEN: I will. Bye, Mum!

4 David is saying goodbye to his fiancée, Ellen, who is going to work in Paris for a few months. Complete their farewell conversation with *will*, *'ll* or *won't*.

DAVID: Promise you'll write!

ELLEN: I [1] *'ll* write every day!

DAVID: And you [2] *won't* forget to phone when you arrive.

ELLEN: No, I [3] *won't.* I [4] *'ll* phone as soon as I get to Paris.

DAVID: Anyway, have a wonderful time.

ELLEN: I'm sure I [5] *will.* Oh, I almost forgot, my houseplants! I hope they [6] *won't* die.

DAVID: Don't worry. I [7] *'ll* water them. And every time I do, I [8] *'ll* think of you!

Unit 12

GRAMMAR: quantity pronouns

Properties in France

COTTAGES	1	2	3	4	5
running water	✓	✓	✓	✓	✓
electricity	✓	✓	✓	✓	
a washing machine		✓	✓		
a telephone		✓	✓	✓	
central heating					
a fridge		✓	✓	✓	✓

1 Look at the chart showing the facilities available in some holiday cottages in France. Write about the facilities, using *all, most, some, not many* and *none (of them)*.

1 *All of them have running water*
2 *Most of them have electricity*
3 *Not many of them have a washing machine*
4 *Some of them have a telephone*
5 *None of them have central heating*
6 *Most of them have a fridge*

WRITING

2 You are staying in cottage number 4. Complete the letter to a friend.

Dear *Anna*

We're spending a few days in France. We are staying in a French 'gite' – a sort of country cottage. It's quite primitive. We've got ¹ *running water* and ² *electricity* but there isn't a ³ *fridge*. A few of the cottages have got a ⁴ *central heating* but ours hasn't. But it has got a ⁵ .... Of course there isn't any ⁶ .... but that doesn't matter as the weather is so good. In fact ⁷ .... of the cottages has central heating. I hope all's well with you. Best wishes,

....

GRAMMAR: prepositions

3 Complete the sentences with the correct prepositions from the box.

| at (x3) | from | in (x2) | to (x3) | of |

1 He's still ...*at*... school.
2 I'm moving .... a different part of town.
3 I met him .... work.
4 He escaped .... prison last week.
5 I found the bag .... a doorway.
6 I'd like a chance .... earn a bit of money.
7 .... the end, he found a good job.
8 She prefers working outside .... working in an office.
9 She left home .... sixteen.
10 Thousands .... children leave home every year.

22

Unit 13

COMMUNICATION: suggestions

1 You and your friends are planning a barbecue. Use the notes below to ask for suggestions.

1. how many people to invite?
2. where to have the barbecue?
3. what to have to eat?
4. which supermarket to go to?
5. when to get the food?
6. what time to ask people to come?

A: 1 *How many people shall we invite?*
B: About twenty will be enough.
A: Yes, that's about right. 2 ....
B: Let's have it on the beach.
A: O.K. 3 ....
B: Why don't we have frankfurters? They're easy to cook.
A: Good idea. 4 ....
B: The best one is Banco.
A: Yes, you're right. 5 ....
B: Let's get it on Saturday morning. It'll be fresher then.
A: Fine. 6 ....
B: Let's ask them to come at about six.

2 Make conversations.

1 A: What/do this evening?
  B: go to the cinema/get a video?
A: *What shall we do this evening?*
B: *Why don't we go to the cinema?*
A: *No, I don't want to go to the cinema.*
B: *What about getting a video?*
A: O.K. That's not a bad idea.

2 What/eat tonight?
  make a curry/get some fish and chips?
A: *What shall we eat tonight?*
B: *Why don't we make a curry?*
A: *No, I don't want make a curry.*
B: *What about getting some fish and chips?*
A: O.K. Let's do that instead.

3 What/give Tom for his sixteenth birthday?
  give him a book/get him a video cassette?
A: *What shall we give Tom for his sixteenth birth...*
B: *Why don't we give him a book?*
A: ....
B: ....
A: Good idea. Can you buy it?

GRAMMAR: direct and indirect objects

3 Rewrite the sentences using a pronoun as in the example.

1 I gave ten pounds to the people from 'Greenpeace'.
I gave them ten pounds.

2 Have you shown the photos to John?
Have you shown him the photos?

3 They're going to buy a new bike for Susie.
....

4 I think we'll get an electric razor for my father.
....

5 Could you offer a cup of tea to the visitors?
....

6 I forgot to send a cheque to my brother.
....

Unit 14

GRAMMAR: present perfect with *just*, *already*, *still* and *yet*

1 Complete the conversation between a businessman and a receptionist, using the present perfect tense of the verbs in brackets.

RECEPTIONIST: Can I help you, sir?

MAN: Yes, my name's Nelson. I arrived here an hour ago to see the manager. It's now two o'clock and I (still/not/see) ¹ *still haven't seen* him!

RECEPTIONIST: I'll give him a ring, Mr Nelson. Perhaps you'd like a cup of coffee while you're waiting?

MAN: I (already/have) ² .... two cups.

Five minutes later

RECEPTIONIST: I (just/speak) ³ .... to the manager.

MAN: Good.

RECEPTIONIST: He says he'll see you at two thirty.

MAN: Two thirty!

RECEPTIONIST: The manager (not/finish) ⁴ .... his lunch yet.

MAN: Oh, really!

RECEPTIONIST: (you/have) ⁵ .... your lunch yet, Mr Nelson?

MAN: No, I (have) ⁶ ....

RECEPTIONIST: Well, why don't you go and have a sandwich and come back a bit later?

MAN: No, thank you. I'm leaving. Let me tell you, I (never/meet) ⁷ .... such an inefficient organisation in all my life!

WRITING

2 Rearrange the lines to write a letter which Cathy sent from the airport. Write the letter in your notebook. Start with C.

A Mum's flight to arrive from Athens. It
B arrived. I've been at the airport now for
C Dear Mike,
   I'm writing this in the airport.
D two hours and I've already had four
E yet but I'll do that next week.
F cups of tea and a large glass of
G was due at 6.15 but it still hasn't
H orange juice! By the way, I haven't
I Best wishes,
   Cathy
J collected the photos from our holiday
K I'm waiting for

★ ★ ★ Joke ★ ★ ★

DENTIST: Stop screaming! I haven't touched your tooth yet.
BARRY: I know, but you're standing on my foot.

24

Unit 15

GRAMMAR: past continuous

1 Write questions and answers for each picture.

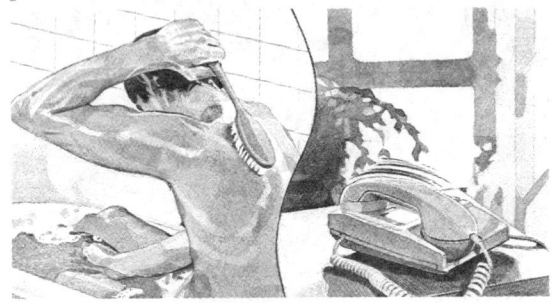

1 telephone ring/have bath
What was he doing when the telephone rang? He was having a bath.

2 police arrive/watch television
....
....

3 a lorry drive on to the pavement/wait for a bus
....
....

4 lights go out/have dinner
....
....

5 man steal her purse/buy fruit
....
....

6 start to rain/play tennis
....
....

2 Complete the text using the past simple or past continuous tense of the verbs in brackets.

IT'S A FUNNY WORLD!

A friend of mine, who is blind, (wait) ¹..*was waiting*.. at the bus stop one day with her guide dog. The bus (be) ²............... late and a man, who (also stand) ³............... in the queue, (ask) ⁴............... his companion the time. My blind friend, who (bend down) ⁵............... at the time to adjust the dog's harness, (consult) ⁶............... her Braille watch and (call) ⁷............... over her shoulder: 'It's five past eight.' In a surprised voice, the man (whisper) ⁸............... to his companion: 'Goodness me, her dog can tell the time!'

VOCABULARY

3 Complete the text using the correct form of the words in the box in the appropriate places.

breathe	towel	flame	fire	put out
spread	destroy	burn	smoke	
rescue				

FIRE DESTROYS HOUSE
By Jane Kernahan

THIRTY-SEVEN-year-old Richard Dickson had a nasty shock when he got home yesterday. To his horror, his house was on ¹*fire* and ²............ were coming out of the windows. He grabbed his garden hose but wasn't able to ³............... the fire before it began to ⁴............... through the whole house.

Mr Dickson then remembered his cat in the kitchen. He ran inside to ⁵............... it but the fire was still ⁶............... On his way out, he couldn't ⁷............... because of the ⁸............... and he collapsed in the doorway. Fortunately firefighters arrived and covered him in wet ⁹............... Although the fire was put out, it ¹⁰............... most of the house. Last night Mr Dickson was said to be comfortable in hospital.

Listening and speechwork 11–15

LISTENING

Would you fall in love with this man?

This is the face of the perfect man according to an American psychologist. He showed 250 American women thousands of photographs of men's faces, and he believes he has found the face all American women think is perfect. But has he?

We decided to find out what women from different countries think about their American sisters' ideal man.

1 Listen to the five interviews and tick the chart where appropriate.

Opinions	Erika from Germany	Sue from England	Clara from Italy	Jean from the USA	Rosa from Brazil
1 He is the ideal man.					
2 He is attractive.					
3 He is too perfect.	✓				
4 His eyes are nice.					
5 His nose is too small.					
6 Character is important.	✓				

2 Listen again to check your chart. Then complete the sentences about the survey with the words in the box.

all   a few   most   none   one   some

1 ...*None*... of them thinks he is the ideal man.
2 .... of them thinks he is attractive.
3 .... of them think he is too perfect.
4 .... of them like his eyes.
5 .... of them think his nose is too small.
6 .... of them think character is important.

3 Listen to three conversations and circle the sentence which best explains what is going on in each conversation.

CONVERSATION 1
a) The man has just dropped a sandwich.
b) The man has just torn up a letter by mistake.
c) The man has just broken a vase.

CONVERSATION 2
a) The boy has already seen the film.
b) The boy saw the film with the girl.
c) The boy hasn't seen the film yet.

CONVERSATION 3
a) The girl has just finished the book.
b) The girl hasn't started the book yet.
c) The girl has just started reading the book.

ORAL EXERCISES

4 Promise to do things.

T: When are you going to buy the tickets?
S: *I'll buy them tomorrow.*

1 tomorrow
2 now
3 this evening
4 at the weekend
5 next week
6 soon

5 Talk about completed activities.

T: You could write to John.
S: *I've already written to him.*

1 write
2 phone
3 tell
4 speak
5 read
6 see

6 Talk about past activities.

T: Oh sorry. Were you watching a film?
S: *No, it's O.K. I was only watching the news.*

1 watch the news
2 have a cup of coffee
3 rest
4 chat to Ann
5 wash my hands
6 write a letter

PRONUNCIATION

Consonant clusters with 's'
/sk/ skirt   /st/ start   /sm/ smoke
/sn/ snow   /sl/ slow

7 Listen and repeat the words and phrases.

skirt   smoke   snake
school   smile   slow
start   snow   slim
stand

She walked slowly to school.
It started to snow.
She wore a slim skirt.

Consonant sounds
The linking /r/
fa**r a**nd wide

8 Listen and repeat the phrases.

far and wide   brother and sister
here and there   better and better
mother and father   nearer and nearer

STRESS AND INTONATION

Sentence stress
○ ○ ○ ○ ○ ○ ○
What was he doing at home?

9 Listen and underline the stressed syllables.

1 What was he doing at home?
2 What were they saying to John?
3 Who were you trying to phone?
4 What was the name of his wife?

Now listen and repeat the questions.

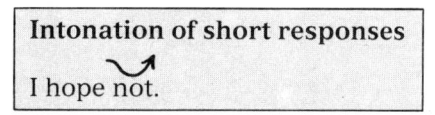

Intonation of short responses
I hope not.

10 Listen to the conversation and repeat the answers.

T1: Do you think we'll have to answer more than four questions in the exam?
T2: I hope not.
S: *I hope not.*

1 I hope not.
2 I think so.
3 I don't think so.
4 I hope not.
5 I hope so.

Unit 16

READING

1 Read the letter to a newspaper and circle the correct answers.

> Dear Sir,
>
> We are now about to enter the twenty-first century but many young people today still have the same eating habits they had twenty years ago. They still eat too much fat and sugar because they eat too many crisps, snacks and sweets.
>
> I know that some schools try to give students healthy meals at lunch time but there are still plenty of schools which serve mostly hamburgers and chips!
>
> Children certainly do not have enough healthy food in their diet. I cannot understand why this is so, when I always see plenty of fresh fruit and vegetables in the shops.
>
> There is, of course, another issue – the food that we throw away. Every day school kitchens in Britain throw away enough food to feed an Ethiopian village for a year! Isn't it time we did something about this?
>
> Yours faithfully,
>
> C. Hickley
> Oxford

1. a) Children's eating habits have got better.
   b) Children's eating habits have got worse.
   c) **Children's eating habits have stayed the same.**

2. a) Children are not getting enough to eat.
   b) Children get too much to eat.
   c) Children are not eating the right food.

3. a) A lot of schools serve healthy food.
   b) Not enough schools serve healthy food.
   c) The students are asking for healthier food.

4. a) Children don't eat enough fruit and vegetables.
   b) Fresh fruit and vegetables are too expensive.
   c) There are not enough fruit and vegetables in the shops.

GRAMMAR: *too much/too many* and *not enough*

2 Complete the sentences about pollution of the planet using *too much*, *too many* or *not enough*.

HOW WE ARE DESTROYING OUR PLANET

1. There are ...*too many*... cars on the roads.
2. We ...*do not*... use ...*enough*... energy from the sun.
3. We use .... plastic.
4. We put .... chemicals into the sea.
5. We use .... electricity.
6. We burn .... coal.
7. We .... use .... wind power.
8. We are destroying .... trees and forests.
9. We .... recycle .... glass and paper.

VOCABULARY

5.00 The Good Life
Still very funny. Will definitely make you laugh.

5.35 Neighbours
Jim is worried about Todd and Melissa's flower business – and guess who's getting married.

6.30 Family Fortunes
Two families compete for some fantastic prizes.

7.00 Wogan
Conversation and entertainment when Terry Wogan talks to Shirley MacLaine and Meryl Streep.

7.30 The Hungry World
This investigation looks at the desperate food shortages in much of t Sahel region of Africa

8.30 City Streets
This exciting New Yo police series is back w 'Terror in Times Squa

9.30 The World This We
A survey of the week events presented by Adrienne West.

3 Complete the sentences with the correct programme title.

1. ...*Family Fortunes is*... a quiz show.
2. .... a 'chat' show.
3. .... a crime series.
4. .... a documentary.
5. .... a soap opera.
6. .... a news programme.
7. .... a comedy show.

29

Unit 17

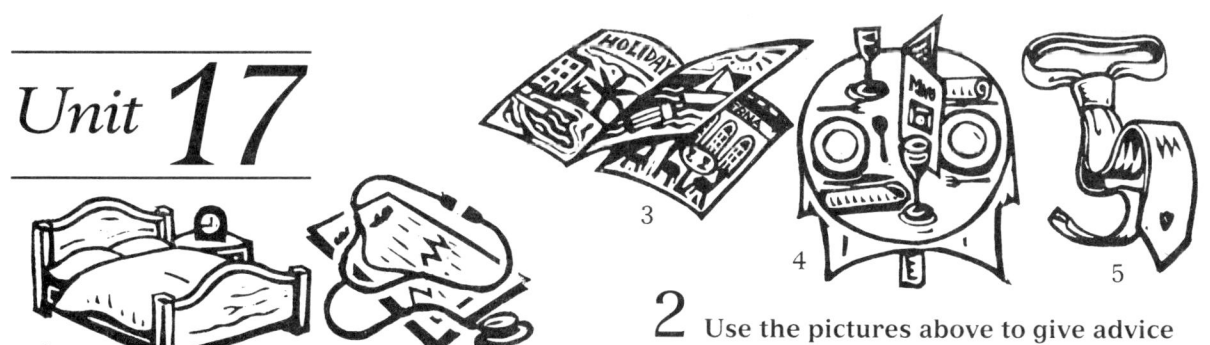

COMMUNICATION: giving advice

1 Write conversations.

1 I want to buy my sister a present to thank her for her help. (How much/I/spend)
How much do you think I should spend?
(about £10)
I think you should spend about £10.

2 My son wants to buy a CD system. (Where/he/go)
Where do you think he should go?
(to the new hi-fi shop in the High Street)
I think he should go to the new hi-fi shop in the High street

3 Sally needs to see a specialist about her bad knee. (Who/she/see)
Who do you think she should see
(Dr Harvey)
I think they should see Dr. Harvey stay with us.

4 John and Sue can't find anywhere to stay in London. (What/they/do)
What do you think they should do?
(stay with us)
I think they should stay with us.

5 We need to get a visa for the USA. (When/we/apply)
When do you think we should apply?
(as soon as possible)
I think that you should apply as soon as possible

6 My boss is coming to supper tomorrow. (What/I/call him)
What do you think I should call him?
(by his first name)
I think you should call by his first name

2 Use the pictures above to give advice using *ought to* and one of the verbs in the box.

| see | go | have | wear | go out |

1 I'm tired.
I think you ought to go to bed early.

2 I've got a pain in my back again.
I think you ought to see a doctor

3 I'm feeling stressed.
I think you ought to have a holiday

4 It's our wedding anniversary today.
I think you ought to go out to some restaurant

5 I'm going for an interview this morning.
I think you ought to wear a tie

3 Clare is going to Spain for a week. Her mother is giving her advice. Complete their conversation with one of the words in the box.

| ought | should | oughtn't | shouldn't |

MOTHER: How much money are you going to take?
CLARE: I don't need very much. I'm only going for a week.
MOTHER: Well, you ¹ *ought* to get some pesetas from the bank before you go.
CLARE: I'll do that tomorrow morning.
MOTHER: You ² *oughtn't* to leave it too late, you know.
CLARE: You ³ *shouldn't* worry so much. I can take care of myself.
MOTHER: I know. What time are you leaving tomorrow?
CLARE: The flight leaves at 3.30.
MOTHER: Well, I think you ⁴ *should* go to bed now and get a good night's sleep.
CLARE: Mum! I'm grown up now!

30

Unit 18

READING

1 You are the receptionist at the Strand Hotel. Read the hotel information sheet and answer the guests' questions.

The Strand Hotel
INFORMATION

BREAKFAST A full breakfast is available in the coffee lounge on the first floor from 7.30 a.m. to 10.00 a.m. Please remember that smoking is not allowed in the breakfast area.

LUNCH AND DINNER The hotel restaurant is on the fifth floor. A buffet lunch is available between 12 noon and 2.30 p.m. and a full four-course dinner from 7.00 p.m. to 11.00 p.m. Guests are welcome to wear casual dress at lunch time but we request formal dress at dinner.

ROOM SERVICE If you need snacks or drinks during the day or night, please call Room Service (dial 02).

DISCO NINETIES This is situated next to the bar on the ground floor. Children under 14 must have an adult with them.

DEPARTURE Guests must leave their rooms by noon on the day of departure.

1 Where do you serve breakfast?
In the coffee lounge on the first floor.

2 What time do you stop serving breakfast?
At 10.00 a.m.

3 Which floor is the disco on?
On the ground floor.

4 What number do I dial for room service?
Dial 02.

5 Can I wear jeans in the restaurant at lunch?
Yes, you can.

GRAMMAR: *(not) allowed to/have to*

2 Complete the statements about the Strand Hotel, using *allowed to*, *not allowed to* and *have to*.

1 You **are not allowed to** smoke in the breakfast area.
2 You **are allowed to** wear casual clothes in the restaurant at lunchtime.
3 You **are not allowed to** wear jeans at dinner.
4 You **are allowed to** dial 02 to get Room Service.
5 You **are not allowed to** go in to the disco alone if you are fourteen or under.
6 You **have to** leave you room by noon on your day of departure.

GRAMMAR: *not + adjective + enough*

3 Combine the two sentences to make one using *not + adjective + enough + to*.

1 The sea is not very warm. You can't swim in it.
The sea is not warm enough to swim in.

2 The child isn't very old. He can't travel alone.
The child is not old enough to travel alone.

3 It's not very cold. I don't want to turn the central heating on.
It is not cold enough to turn the central heating on.

4 She's not very well. She can't go out.
She is not well enough to go out.

5 The oven isn't very hot. You can't put the meat in yet.
The oven is not hot enough to put the meat in yet.

6 He isn't very intelligent. He won't get the job.
He is not intelligent enough to get the job.

★ ★ ★ Joke ★ ★ ★

DRIVING INSTRUCTOR: Slow down, please.
LEARNER: I'm only doing 25 miles an hour. You're allowed to do 30 in this area.
DRIVING INSTRUCTOR: Yes, but not on the pavement.

Unit 19

COMMUNICATION: reminders, advice and warnings

1 Write the correct response *I will* or *I won't* next to each phrase.

1 Don't forget to write! — *I won't.*
2 Send me a postcard! — I will
3 Make sure you check the oil. — I will
4 Watch out for pickpockets! — I will
5 Don't do anything silly! — I won't
6 Remember to phone Sally before you go. — I will
7 Don't lose your key. — I won't
8 Have a nice holiday. — I will
9 Be careful! — I will
10 Always lock the door after you. — I will

2 Complete the instructions to kitchen staff in a hotel kitchen with *Always*, *Never* or *Make sure*.

1 *Always* wear a hat.
2 Never leave any food out of the fridge over night.
3 Always wash your hands before you touch food.
4 Make sure you clean up immediately if you drop food or drink on the floor.
5 Never keep salads longer than one day.
6 Make sure you don't use dirty knives or spoons.
7 Always wash fresh fruit before serving it.

VOCABULARY: containers

3 Write the correct word from the box under each picture.

purse	tin	bag
handbag	suitcase	
wallet	box	pocket

1 *handbag* 
2 suitcase
3 bag
4 wallet
5 pocket
6 purse
7 box
8 tin

32

READING

4 Read the article, then write *Right* or *Wrong* for each situation.

WHAT TO DO IF YOU HAVE AN ACCIDENT

- Always stop if you have an accident, even if the accident is very minor.
- Make sure you exchange details with the other driver, e.g. name, address, telephone number, the car registration number and insurance details.
- Remember to note the time, date and place of the accident.
- Never say that the accident was your fault. Only give information which is necessary.
- Try to get the names and addresses of any witnesses who saw the accident.

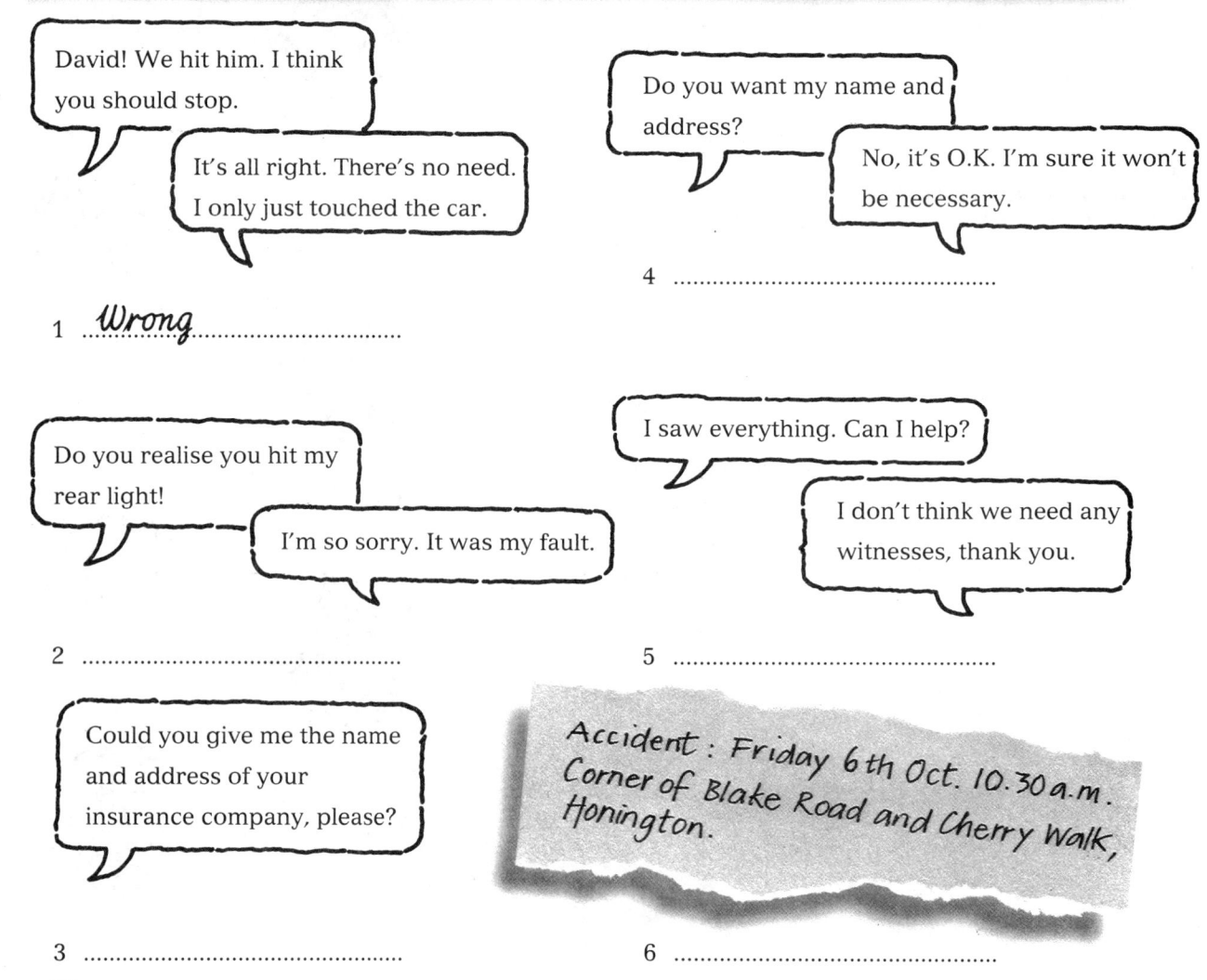

David! We hit him. I think you should stop.

It's all right. There's no need. I only just touched the car.

1 *Wrong*

Do you want my name and address?

No, it's O.K. I'm sure it won't be necessary.

4 ....

Do you realise you hit my rear light!

I'm so sorry. It was my fault.

2 ....

I saw everything. Can I help?

I don't think we need any witnesses, thank you.

5 ....

Could you give me the name and address of your insurance company, please?

3 ....

Accident: Friday 6th Oct. 10.30 a.m. Corner of Blake Road and Cherry Walk, Honington.

6 ....

Unit 20

David Hockney

A Bigger Splash (1975)

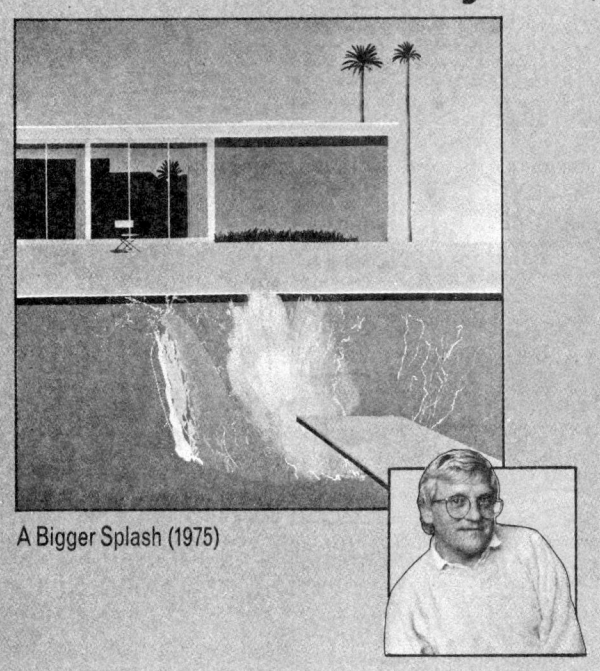

DAVID HOCKNEY, one of Britain's most popular artists, was born in Bradford, Yorkshire, in 1937. After leaving Bradford Grammar School at the age of eighteen, he went to Bradford School of Art and after that to the famous Royal College of Art in London, where he was one of the best students of his generation. Then, at the age of twenty-five, he became a lecturer at Maidstone College of Art, not far from London.

During his time at art school, he decided that he did not want to paint abstract art so he developed a more 'representational' style, using strong, light colours.

One year after joining Maidstone College of Art, he had his first exhibition, which was a great success. During the sixties he became world-famous as a popular artist. In 1964 he moved to California in the USA, where he now lives permanently.

One of Hockney's most famous paintings is 'A Bigger Splash', which he painted in 1975. The theme of swimming pools appears in several of his paintings because he likes the effect of movement and sunlight on blue water.

As well as painting, Hockney is also a talented photographer. In 1985 he won a first prize for photography. He has also designed costumes and sets for opera and ballet.

READING

1 Read the text about the British artist, David Hockney and complete his biographical details with a date or a fact.

1937	
1955	
1957	Went to the Royal College of Art.
1962	
	Had his first exhibition.
1964	
	Painted 'A Bigger Splash'.
1985	

GRAMMAR: *during*, *while* and *for*

2 Complete the sentences with *during*, *while* or *for*.

1 I read the whole of *War and Peace* ...**while**... I was ill.
2 My grandfather was in the navy ...during... the war.
3 I waited in the rain ...for... ten minutes and then I left.
4 Your letter came ...while... I was having breakfast.
5 The phone rang twice ...during... lunch.
6 She worked in Paris ...for... five years.
7 It was awful. He couldn't stop coughing ...during... the concert.
8 We usually go out on Saturday night but we don't go out ...during... the week.

34

GRAMMAR: before/after + ing

3 When Josh returns home from a trip, he usually does things in the same order. Write sentences to show what he did when he came back from Amsterdam. Link the events with *After . . . ing*.

1 First he read his post.
2 After reading *his post, he listened to the news.*
3 ....
4 ....
5 ....
6 ....

phone Eva — *read his post* — *listen to the news* — *make a cup of tea* — *have a shower* — *unpack his clothes*

4 Write sentences to say in which order you usually do things when you return from a holiday.

1 *I usually unpack my clothes before/after reading my post.*
2 ....
3 ....
4 ....

5 Complete the sentences about yourself.

1 Before going to bed, I always ....
2 I always ....
   ....
   before going to the dentist.
3 After spending a lot of money, I often ....
   ....
4 I like ....
   ....
   after working all day.
5 Before having my first cup of coffee of the day, I ....
   ....
6 I usually ....
   ....
   before guests arrive.
7 After having a shower in the morning, I ....
   ....

Listening and speechwork 16–20

LISTENING

1 Philip, a student, twisted his ankle when he went skiing. Some weeks later he went to see his doctor. Listen to their conversation and circle the correct answers.

1 Philip twisted his ankle
  a) three months ago.
  b) three weeks ago. *(circled)*
  c) a month ago.

2 Philip wants the doctor's permission to
  a) play football.
  b) go skiing.
  c) walk on his ankle.

3 The doctor tells him he should wait
  a) six weeks more.
  b) four weeks more.
  c) one or two weeks more.

4 The doctor then tells him he should
  a) start exercising the ankle.
  b) rest the ankle.
  c) stop exercising the ankle.

5 The doctor tells the story of someone who played football very soon after an accident and
  a) twisted his ankle again.
  b) broke his ankle.
  c) discovered that his ankle didn't hurt.

ORAL EXERCISES

2 Make complaints.

S: I'm not going to drive to London.
T: Why?
S: *There's too much traffic on the roads.*

1 traffic on the roads
2 salt in it
3 chat shows on it
4 violence there
5 problems with it
6 people on it

3 Give advice.

T: I'm tired.
S: *I think you should go to bed early.*

1 go to bed early
2 get a new bed
3 tell your boss
4 go by train
5 complain to the waiter
6 stop smoking

4 Criticise people.

T: He drives much too fast.
S: *I know. I think he ought to drive more slowly.*

1 slow
2 careful
3 frequent
4 slow
5 clear
6 often

5 Tell people not to do things.

T: I'll leave the car in front of this house.
S: *Excuse me, I'm afraid you're not allowed to park here.*

1 park
2 bring dogs
3 wear shorts
4 take photographs
5 smoke
6 eat

PRONUNCIATION

Aspiration after /p/, /t/ and /k/
/p/ pain   /t/ take   /k/ cost

6 Listen and tick the word you hear.

1 pack ...✓.... back ....
2 too .... do ....
3 curl .... girl ....
4 tie .... die ....
5 pet .... bet ....
6 came .... game ....

7 Listen and repeat the words and phrases.

pack   tired   come
too   Paris   buy

The girls are coming to Paris.
Pat posted the parcel.
He's packing to go to Paris.

Double consonants
part time   midday

8 Listen and repeat the words and phrases.

midday   big girl
part time   hard day
nice seats   old dog
ten names

STRESS AND INTONATION

Sentence stress
○ ○ ○ ○
Never go alone

9 Listen and underline the stressed syllables.

1 Never go alone.
2 Always take a bus.
3 Don't go out at night.
4 Always close your bag.

Now listen and repeat the sentences.

Intonation of neutral and excited responses
↗Yes   ↘YES

10 Listen and repeat each of these words in two different ways.

Yes.   No.   Thank you.   Why.

Now listen to four short conversations and repeat the responses when you hear them. Try to say them in exactly the same way.

T1: Are you going home now?
T2: Yes.
S: *Yes.*

1 Yes.   3 Thank you.
2 No.   4 Why?

Unit 21

GRAMMAR: may/might/going to

1 Eva is thinking about her plans for the evening. Complete the paragraph below using *may* or *going to* and a verb phrase.

1. stop at the cinema ✓
2. buy a newspaper ?
3. telephone Josh ✓
4. do my laundry ✓ (orange)
5. get some fish and chips ?
6. watch TV ?

On her way home from college, Eva ¹ *is going to stop at the cinema* to see which films are on. She ² *may buy a newspaper*, too. When she gets home, she ³ *is going to telephone Josh* to find out if he wants to go out later. Then, she ⁴ *is going to do her laundry*. Later on, she ⁵ *might get some fish and chips* from the shop down the road. After that, she ⁶ *might watch TV*. One of her favourite programmes is on tonight.

2 Answer questions about Eva's plans using short form answers.

1. Is Eva going to stop at the cinema? — *Yes, she is*
2. Is she going to buy a newspaper? — *She may*
3. Is she going to telephone Josh? — *Yes, she is*
4. Is she going to do her laundry? — *Yes, she is*
5. Is she going to get some fish and chips? — *She might*
6. Is she going to watch TV? — *She might*

READING

3 Read the text and write *True* (T) or *False* (F) for each of the statements below.

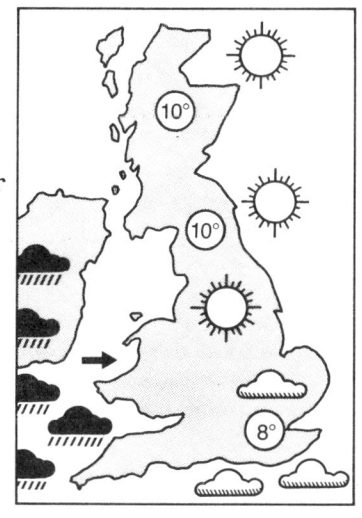

The forecast for tomorrow is much cooler, with temperatures dropping from fifteen to about eight degrees Celsius. In the south-east it will be cloudy with the possibility of rain during the afternoon and evening. In the north of England and Scotland, however, it will stay bright and sunny with temperatures reaching a maximum of ten degrees Celsius. The forecast for the next few days is not so good. There will be rain and possibly some stormy weather coming in from the Atlantic.

1. The weather will be warmer tomorrow. [F]
2. It might rain in the south-east later. [T]
3. It will be wetter (more) in the north of England than in the south-east. [F]
4. The temperature in Scotland might reach 15°C. [F]
5. There may be some storms in the next few days. [T]

WRITING

4 Read the extract from a letter. Then, in your notebook, write a similar paragraph to a friend who is coming to stay for a week. You are planning to go to a wedding and possibly to stay with a friend who has a beach house near the sea.

> That reminds me about clothes and things. You'll definitely need something warm to wear because it gets cold at night. Also you might need some strong shoes because we may go walking one weekend. Looking forward to seeing you.
> Best wishes,
> Jo

38

Unit 22

GRAMMAR: *ask/tell somebody to do something*

1 You are moving house and you are asking a friend to give people some messages. Read the notes below and then write your requests, using *ask*.

> 1 Lorry driver - Park in the street opposite the house.
> 2 Removal men - Put the books in the sitting room.
> 3 My mother - Buy some bread, butter and milk for the weekend.
> 4 My father - Bring some chairs on Sunday morning.
> 5 Eileen - Look after the cat for a week.
> 6 Bill - Tell the post office our new address.

1 *Can you ask the lorry driver to park in the street opposite the house?*
2 *Can you ask the Removal men to put the ...*
3 *Can you ask ~~that~~ my mother to by some*
4 *Can you ask my father to bring*
5 ....
6 ....

2 You work for a small theatre company but you are ill. You ask a colleague to give instructions to a student, Silvia, on her first day at work. Use the verb *tell* with the instructions below to write your requests to your colleague.

> - arrive an hour before the performance
> - don't open the doors until 7 p.m.
> - collect all the tickets at the door
> - show the people to their seats
> - don't allow people to take drinks into the theatre
> - don't leave before the end of the performance

1 *Could you tell Silvia to arrive an hour before the performance?*
2 *Could you tell her not to open the doors until 7 p.m.?*
3 *Could you tell her to collect all the tickets*
4 *Could you tell her to show the people*
5 *Could you tell her not to allow people*
6 ....

VOCABULARY

3 Write the items under an appropriate verb, following the example. Use each item once only.

a plate	a stereo	a glass	a TV
a window	a cup	a bottle	a sweater
a letter	a light		

TURN ON	WASH	OPEN
a stereo	a glass	a window
a TV	a bottle	a bottle
a light	a sweater	a cup
	a cup	a letter
	a plate	

Unit 23

GRAMMAR: stative verb + adjective

1 Complete the conversations using the correct verb and adjective together.

VERB	ADJECTIVE
taste	frightened
smell	soft
sound	delicious
look	bad
feel	upset
seem	salty

1. A: Come on, Smokey. Oh dear, she doesn't want to come.
   B: She _seems frightened_.

2. A: I'm going to cook goulash tonight. It's made with beef, tomatoes, onions and lots of paprika. Have you ever eaten it before?
   B: No, never, but it _sounds delicious_.

3. A: We ought to throw this milk away.
   B: Why?
   A: Because I think it _smells bad_.
   B: Really? It smells O.K. to me.

4. A: The goulash is almost ready. I'll just try it. Oh dear, it _tastes_ very _salty_.
   B: Let me try it. Oh, yes, you're right!

5. A: Look, this is my brother.
   B: Why does he _look upset_?
   A: Well, he got his exam results that day!

6. A: Feel this one, madam, it's made of Scottish wool.
   B: Oh, yes. I like the colour and it _feels_ very _soft_. Is it expensive?

40

GRAMMAR: stative verb + like

2 Use the pictures below to write questions about the people's appearance. Who do they look like in their family?

Polly ✓   sister ✓   father ✗

1 (Polly)
Does Polly look like her sister?
Yes, she does.
Does Polly look like her sister?
No, she doesn't.

Mark ✓   mother ✗   father ✓

2 (Mark)
Does Mark look like his mother?
Yes, he does.
Does Mark look like his father?
No, he doesn't.

Sue ✓   sister ✗   mother ✓

3 (Sue)
Does Sue look like her mother?
Yes, she does.
Does Sue look like her sister?
No, she doesn't.

COMMUNICATION

3 Complete the conversation below using the correct questions from the box.

> What sports does she like?
> How's your mother?
> What does she look like?
> What would she like?
> What's she like?

RUTH: My American cousin is coming to stay on Saturday.
CLARE: Really! [1] *What's she like?*
RUTH: She's very nice and lots of fun.
CLARE: [2] *What*
RUTH: Well, she's tall with brown eyes and she's got short blonde hair. She's very sporty. I think I'll take her to the sports club while she's here.
CLARE: Good idea! [3] *What sports does she like*
RUTH: Oh, swimming, tennis, volleyball.
CLARE: By the way, [4] *How's your mother*
RUTH: Oh, she's fine, thanks. She had a bit of a cold last week but she's better now. In fact it's her birthday next week.
CLARE: Is it? I'd like to get her a present. [5] *What's she like*
RUTH: Perhaps a scarf or something. I'm sure she'd like that.

41

Unit 24

READING AND GRAMMAR:
could/must/can't

1 Read about the three people on the right and say who you think the items belong to, using *could*, *must* or *can't*.

1 a walking stick
   It can't be Melissa's but it could be Alan's or Joan's.
   CLUE: It has a hospital label on it.
   It must be Joan's.

2 a camera
   It can't be Alan's but could be Melissa's
   CLUE: It's a modern Nikon camera with a zoom lens.
   It must be Joan's

3 a typewriter
   It can't be Alan's

   CLUE: It's a modern, electric typewriter.
   It must be Joan's

4 a personal stereo

   CLUE: There's a 'Mozart' cassette in it.

5 trainers

   CLUE: They're a man's size 10.

MELISSA IS A STUDENT. She is in her last year at college. She hasn't got very tidy handwriting so she usually types her essays. In her spare time she goes jogging and plays tennis. She doesn't like taking photographs. In the evening she enjoys listening to music. Her favourite type of music is rock music.

ALAN IS A VERY SUCCESSFUL PHOTOGRAPHER. He doesn't like typing and writes all his letters long-hand. He lives in Cornwall by the sea. In his spare time he likes sailing and going for long walks in the country. He loves classical music and listens to music as often as possible. He's got an excellent personal stereo so he likes listening when he relaxes, especially when he is walking or sailing.

JOAN IS A DETECTIVE STORY WRITER. She types everything on a very old typewriter. She doesn't like modern electrical machines like word processors. Everything in her house is old. Her hobbies are collecting books, old cameras and ornaments. She doesn't go out much at the moment because she's had an accident and hurt her leg.

WRITING

2 Read the note below. Then, in your notebook, write a similar note to some friends. You left your glasses in their flat at the weekend. Say you are sure they are somewhere in the bedroom and suggest some possible places, e.g. on the bedside table/in one of the drawers/by the washbasin.

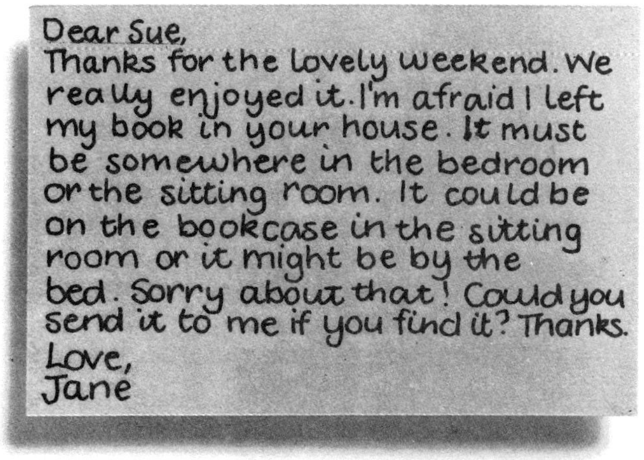

Dear Sue,
Thanks for the lovely weekend. We really enjoyed it. I'm afraid I left my book in your house. It must be somewhere in the bedroom or the sitting room. It could be on the bookcase in the sitting room or it might be by the bed. Sorry about that! Could you send it to me if you find it? Thanks.
Love,
Jane

Unit 25

GRAMMAR: reported requests with *ask* and *tell*

1 Report Josh's requests.

Please put your coats on the rack.

1 He asked us to put our coats on the rack.

Please don't leave any bags on the coach.

2 He asked us not to leave any bags on the coach.

Please don't smoke on the coach.

3 He asked us not to smoke on the coach.

Please be back at the hotel by 3 p.m.

4 He asked us to be back at the hotel by 3 p.m.

Please don't leave anything valuable in your rooms.

5 He asked us to not to leave anything valuable in rooms.

Please bring your tickets for the Van Gogh exhibition.

6 He asked us to bring tickets for the Van Gogh exhibition.

Please don't forget to collect your passports from the hotel reception desk.

7 He asked us not to forget to collect passports from hotel reception desk.

2 Report the teacher's commands.

1 'Be quiet and sit down!'.
He told them to be quiet and sit down.

2 'Don't shout or push.'
He told them not to shout or push.

3 'Don't put your feet on the seats.'
He told them not to put

4 'Put all your rubbish in the bins.'
He told them to put

5 'Don't sing so loudly.'
He told them not to sing so loudly

6 'Please don't throw your chewing gum on the floor.'
He told them not to throw chewing gum on the floor

43

3 Read the reported requests and commands. Change them to direct speech and use them to complete the dialogue.

1 Tom asked Sue not to phone him at work.
2 Sue asked Tom to give her Stewart's telephone number.
3 Sue asked Tom to look in his address book.
4 Tom told Sue to wait a moment.
5 Sue asked Tom to give her the number.
6 Sue told Tom not to be angry.

TOM: Hello. Tom Peters speaking.
SUE: Hi, Tom. It's me, Sue.
TOM: Oh! Hello, Sue. Listen, ¹ *please don't phone me at work*. The boss doesn't like us using the phone for personal calls.
SUE: Sorry, Tom but it's really important. ² ....
TOM: I'm sorry, Sue, I haven't got it.
SUE: Are you sure? ³ ....
TOM: O.K. ⁴ .... Oh yes, here it is.
SUE: Great! ⁵ ....
TOM: It's 071 695 745.
SUE: Thanks. ⁶ .... I won't ring you at work again.
TOM: That's O.K. It's just that our boss is in a bad mood today. Bye.

GRAMMAR: *want somebody to do something*

4 Complete the responses using the cues.

1 I don't want to walk home alone in the dark.
(come with you?)
Do you want me to come with you?

2 What do you want John to do?
(apologise)
I want him to apologise.

3 Mum, I'm going to a party this evening.
All right, but I (be back by midnight)
....

4 What do you want the builders to do with their rubbish?
(take it away)
....

5 I have to go home now.
(give you a lift?)
Do you ....

6 Shall I tell Lena you're getting married?
No, (not/to know)
I don't want her to ....

44

Listening and speechwork 21–25

LISTENING

1 Listen to part of a quiz show and answer *True* or *False*.

1 There were four teams in the competition. *False*
2 The teams weren't allowed to look during the competition. ....
3 In the quiz, the teams had to eat an orange. ....
4 The teams couldn't guess the answer to all the questions. ....
5 The quizmaster asked the winning team to choose a prize. ....

2 Listen again to the quiz. This time tick the correct answer to each quiz question.

1 a peach	a pear	a passion fruit ✓
2 orange juice	chocolate pudding	cough medicine
3 a ball	an orange	a grapefruit
4 snow	a piece of bread	a white towel
5 a saxophone	a trumpet	a clarinet

ORAL EXERCISES

3 Talk about possible situations.

T: Why isn't Alan here?
S: *I think he may be ill.*

1 be ill
2 be late
3 arrive this weekend
4 take half an hour
5 be angry
6 phone this evening

4 Draw conclusions.

T: Is Mr Harris married?
S: *He can't be married. He must be single.*

1 married/single
2 his wife/his girlfriend
3 25/30
4 Scottish/English
5 his/someone else's

5 Check instructions.

You are going on a trip.

T: Please be at the station at 6 p.m. on Thursday.
S: *What time does he want us to be there?*

1 What time/be there
2 Where/meet him
3 What/bring
4 How much/bring
5 When/pay
6 Who/phone

PRONUNCIATION

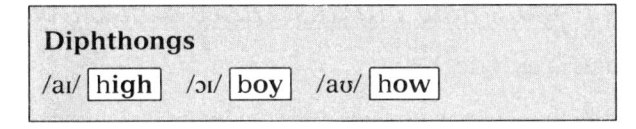

> **Diphthongs**
> /aɪ/ high   /ɔɪ/ boy   /aʊ/ how

6 Listen and repeat the words and phrases.

boy   how   neither
why   noise allowed

Why are the boys making such a loud noise?
Neither of the boys is allowed to go out.

> **Double affricate consonants**
> oran**ge j**uice

7 Listen and repeat the phrases.

orange juice   huge joke
large chicken   large church
orange jacket   not much chance

STRESS AND INTONATION

> **Sentence stress**
> o o O o o O
> Can you <u>tell</u> him to <u>wait</u>?

8 Listen and underline the stressed syllables.

1 Can you tell him to wait?
2 Can you ask her to leave?
3 Could you show us the way?
4 Can you tell her I'll come?

Now listen and repeat the requests.

> **Intonation of interested responses**
> Oh, really?

9 Listen to the conversation and repeat the responses.

T1: We went to the theatre last night.
T2: Oh, really?
S: *Oh, really?*

1 Oh, really?
2 Oh, yes?
3 No?
4 Oh, did you?
5 Oh, are they?

Unit 26

GRAMMAR: question tags

1 Chief Inspector Baker is interviewing Bob Martins about a murder. He is checking some facts. Complete the questions with an appropriate tag.

1 Now, Mr Martins. You're twenty-six, *aren't you?*
2 And you live at 16, High Road, Kensington, *don't you?*
3 Right. On Friday 24th November you left work at 6 o'clock, *didn't you?*
4 But you didn't catch the train home as usual, *did you?*
5 Your girlfriend was planning to meet you outside the station at 6.25, *wasn't she?*
6 But you weren't there, *were you?*
7 You went to your girlfriend's house and waited for her, *didn't you?*
8 Your girlfriend's neighbours heard a strange noise, *didn't they?*
9 You didn't go home until 7.45, *did you?*
10 I think you've lied to us, *haven't you?*

COMMUNICATION

2 Sue is talking to her friend, Liz. Choose the correct sentences from the box to complete what Sue says.

> But he's been there a lot without you, hasn't he?
> Well, he was there last night with Alix.
> You know Ziggy's Disco, don't you?
> And you've been there with him, haven't you?
> Your boyfriend Mark goes there a lot, doesn't he?
> It's a great place, isn't it?

SUE: *You know Ziggy's Disco, don't you?*
LIZ: Yes, I do.
SUE: *It's a great place, isn't it?*
LIZ: Yes, it's really nice.
SUE: *Your boyfriend Mark goes there a lot, doesn't he?*
LIZ: Yes, he does. Nearly every night.
SUE: *And you've been there with him, haven't you?*
LIZ: Sure, I have. Once or twice.
SUE: *But he's been there a lot without you, hasn't he?*
LIZ: Of course he has. What's the problem?
SUE: *Well, he was there last night with Alix.*
LIZ: So what! They both work there!

PUNCTUATION

3 In your notebook, rewrite the following extract from an informal letter using the correct punctuation. Use full stops, commas, question marks, capital letters, and apostrophes where necessary.

dear karen
you didnt expect a letter from me did you in fact i am writing this in hospital ive broken my leg and ive got to stay in hospital until sunday ive already written to my parents my spanish teacher and jonathan thats not bad is it

Dear Karen,
You didn't expect a letter from me, did you? In fact I'am writing this in hospital. I've broken my leg and I've got to stay in hospital until sunday. I've already written to my parents, my Spanish teacher and Jonathan. That's not bad, is it?

Unit 27

COMMUNICATION

1 Express surprise with a question tag.

1 'Do you see that man wearing sunglasses? Well, that's Tom Cruise.'
   It isn't, is it?

2 'I swim two miles every day.'
   You don't, do you?

3 'My sister is working in Fiji.'
   She isn't, is she?

4 'I can speak Mandarin Chinese.'
   You can't, can you?

5 'My brother won a gold medal for boxing in the last Olympic Games.'
   He didn't, did he?

6 'I've just been to the Sahara Desert for a holiday.'
   You haven't, have you?

7 'John will be very upset.'
   He won't, will he?

2 Match the remarks in the left-hand column with a suitable response.

1 I've won £1,000!
2 Thanks very much!
3 I'll help you with that.
4 I'm terribly sorry.
5 Happy New Year!
6 It says here that a fly has hundreds of eyes.
7 Oh no! We've run out of bread!

a) And the same to you.
b) We haven't, have we?
c) That's interesting.
d) You're welcome.
e) Thanks. That's very kind of you.
f) Good heavens!
g) That's O.K. Don't worry about it.

| 1 | f | 2 | d | 3 | e | 4 | g |
| 5 | a | 6 | c | 7 | b |

VOCABULARY

3 Match the correct word from the box with the dictionary definition.

hole   valuable   sink   priceless   cockpit   cancel   shatter

v to give up a planned activity, event; decide that something will not happen

1 *cancel*

v to go down below the surface, out of sight, or to the bottom (of water)

2 sink

n the part of the plane, small boat or racing car in which the pilot or driver sits

3 cockpit

n an empty space inside something

4 hole

adj of such high value that it cannot be calculated

5 valuable

v to break into very small pieces

6 shatter

adj worth a lot of money

7 priceless

48

Unit 28

GRAMMAR: defining relative clauses omitting who/which

1 Link the sentences with a defining relative clause, omitting *who* or *which* where possible.

1 I know the company. Jack works for it.
I know the company Jack works for.

2 Have you been to the sports shop? It has very expensive trainers.
Have you been to the sports shop which has very expensive trainers.

3 I met a woman. She lives next door to Clare.
I met a woman who lives next door to Clare.

4 We are going to see the new James Bond film. Everybody is talking about it.
We are going to see the new James Bond film which everybody is talking about.

5 Joan reads a lot of books. They tell you how to be a success in business.
Joan reads a lot of books which tell you how to be a success in business.

6 Look! There's the new teacher. I told you about her.
Look! There's the new teacher I told you about.

7 I'm wearing the leather jacket. My mother gave it to me for my birthday.
I'm wearing the leather jacket my mother gave to me for my birthday.

8 Did you meet the man? He won the London Marathon.
Did you meet the man who won the London Marathon.

GRAMMAR: defining and non-defining who/which

2 Complete the following passage with *who* or *which*. Put brackets round (*which*) if it is possible to omit it.

DADDY'S LITTLE GIRL

I took my son, ¹ *who* was one month old, to my parents' house for a visit. We slept in the bedroom ² *(which)* I had when I was a child. At about 11.30 p.m., I was still awake. I heard my mother, ³ *who* was in bed, say to my father: 'It's cold. Make sure the baby has a cover on.'

My father came out of their bedroom, ⁴ *which* was opposite mine. I pretended to be asleep. I wanted to see my father, ⁵ *who* was now a grandfather, in action! He came into the room, but he didn't go near the cot ⁶ *(which)* the baby was sleeping in. Instead, he came over to the bed ⁷ *(which)* I was in and made sure my blanket was covering me before he went back to bed!

VOCABULARY

3 Read the adjectives and circle the odd one out.

1	2	3
unusual	spectacular	useless
different	(frightening)	uncomfortable
(expensive)	exciting	elegant
strange	impressive	(boring)

4	5
pretty	useful ?
(ugly)	dangerous
attractive	difficult
beautiful	tiring

49

Unit 29

GRAMMAR: comparison of adjectives

1 Eva is trying to decide which camera to buy. Compare the cameras above, using *a bit* or *much* and the comparative adjective.

1 (A and B) expensive
   The Ricoh is a bit more expensive than the Olympus.

2 (A and D) big
   The Ricoh is much bigger than the Goldline.

3 (C and B) suitable for beginners
   The Minolta is much more suitable for beginners.

4 (A and D) heavy
   The Ricoh is much heavier than the Goldline.

5 (D and C) easy to carry
   The Goldline is a bit easier to carry than the Minolta.

6 (B and A) small
   The Olympus is a bit smaller than the Ricoh.

7 (D and B) cheap
   The Goldline is much cheaper than the Olympus.

8 (A and C) sophisticated
   The Ricoh is much more sophisticated than the Minolta.

COMMUNICATION

2 Sarah and Mark are comparing different sporting activities. Complete their conversation with *more . . . than, less . . . than, as . . . as* or *the same as*.

SARAH: I've just been hang gliding. It was the most amazing experience I've ever had.

MARK: It's quite a dangerous sport, isn't it?

SARAH: No, not really, It's not (dangerous) ¹ *as dangerous as* flying, or motor racing.

MARK: Motor racing! Now that's a great sport! Have you ever been to a Grand Prix?

SARAH: No! As far as I'm concerned motor racing is even (boring) ² *more boring than* football.

MARK: Well, watching a sport is not ³ *the same as* playing it or doing it. Just watching is much (interesting) ⁴ *less interesting than* taking part.

SARAH: That's true. That's why I enjoy hang gliding, I suppose.
It's (exciting) ⁵ *as exciting as* any other sport I've ever done.

MARK: Well, I suppose we're probably just (crazy) ⁶ *more crazy than* each other!

50

VOCABULARY

3 Complete the crossword.

	1 E	2 A	S	I	3 E	R		4 L		5 A
		A			A		6 F	A	S	T
	7 O	L	D	E	R			R		T
					8 L	O	N	G	E	R
	9 H	P	P	Y				E		A
	E				10 A	S				C
	A		11 M		12 L			13 B	I	T
	14 V	I	O	L	E	N	T			I
	Y		R		S					V
		15 L	E	A	S	T		16 T	H	E

CLUES

Across

1. Russian is a difficult language. Italian is a bit . . . (6)
6. Not slow! (4)
7. She's 25 and he's 23, so she's . . . than him. (5)
8. If A is shorter than B, then B is . . . than A. (6)
9. I smile when I feel like this. (5)
10. I'm not as young . . . I was. (2)
13. What's the difference? I suppose this one's a . . . bigger. (3)
14. Adjective from *violence*. (7)
15. *Many, more, most. Little, less,* . . . (5)
16. . . . most important thing is to be 9 across! (3)

Down

2. Opposite of 9 across. (3)
3. Most people don't like getting up . . . (5)
4. Big. (5)
5. Good looking. (10)
9. If you can't carry something, it's probably too . . . (5)
11. The book was much . . . interesting than I expected. (4)
12. That vase costs £20 but this one is . . . expensive. It's only £15. (4)

51

Unit 30

GRAMMAR: *although, however*

1 Make sentences using *although* and *however*.

1 we haven't got a lot of money/we eat quite well/we don't buy expensive food.

Although we haven't got a lot of money, we eat quite well. However, we don't buy expensive food.

2 I like my job/I know I could find a better one/I don't have time to look for one.

Although I like my job, I know I could find a better one. However, I don't have time to look for one.

3 she is only sixteen/she is quite grown-up/I don't think she should leave school yet.

Although she is only sixteen, she is quite grown-up. However, I don't think she should leave school yet.

4 she speaks some Spanish/she isn't very fluent/she doesn't need Spanish for her job.

Although she speaks some Spanish, she isn't very fluent. However, she doesn't need Spanish for her job.

5 he's lazy/he is, in fact, quite intelligent/he has to work hard to pass his exams.

Although he's lazy, he is, in fact, quite intelligent. However, he has to work hard to pass his exams.

GRAMMAR: linking words

2 Nkomo lives in Kenya. Read about his day and complete the text with the correct linking word from the box.

| however   because   and (x2)   so |
| while   although (x2) |

Nkomo wakes up at 5 o'clock in the morning ¹ *and* makes tea ² *while* his wife prepares breakfast. ³ *Although* he doesn't have a large breakfast, he always has a cup of strong, sweet tea.

Work starts at 6 o'clock ⁴ *and* continues until 12 o'clock. Nobody works after that time ⁵ *because* it gets too hot. Nkomo usually goes to sleep under a tree. ⁶ *However*, after three hours it's time to start work again. His boss gives him food and drink during the day ⁷ *so* he doesn't have to pay extra for his meals. ⁸ *Although* he quite likes his job, he would like his boss to pay him more money.

52

MEET DIMITRI HVOROSTOWVSKY

The young opera star who came from Siberia to conquer the West

YVONNE THOMAS talks to the young singer after his performance in Milan

DIMITRI HVOROSTOWVSKY, who looks like a pop star, but is in fact an opera singer, comes from southern Siberia in the USSR. When he was a boy, his favourite occupation was football but he always had the voice of an angel.

Before he won the TV *Singer of the World* contest, Dimitri lived with his parents in a one-bedroom apartment in Kraseoyarsk in Siberia. His parents still live there, but Dimitri now lives with his wife, Svetlana, just outside Moscow. Dimitri met Svetlana when he went to ballet school as part of his training as an opera singer.

At the moment Dimitri is doing a world tour. Every day his fans send him letters and presents. He can now afford to wear designer clothes but his mother dislikes them. Dimitri enjoys being a famous opera star but he is not always happy. 'I think Italy is wonderful,' says Dimitri, 'but I miss Russia very much.'

READING

3 Read about Dimitri and answer *True, False,* or *Don't know.*

1 Dimitri is a famous opera singer.
   True

2 He likes pop music too.
   Don't know

3 He played football when he was younger.
   True

4 His parents are from Siberia.
   True

5 His wife is a ballet dancer.
   Don't know

6 His mother now buys designer clothes.
   False

7 He would like to live in Italy.
   False

4 Make five statements about Dimitri, starting with *although*.

1 Although Dimitri *looks like* a pop star, he is in fact *an opera singer*.

2 Although his favourite occupation *was football*, he *always had the voice of an angel*.

3 Although his parents *live* in Kraseoyarsk in Siberia, he *now lives just outside Moscow*.

4 Although he can afford *to wear designer clothes*, his mother *dislikes them*.

5 Although he *thinks Italy is* wonderful, he *misses Russia very much*.

Listening and speechwork 26–30

LISTENING

1 Listen to the conversation and write *Yes* (Y), *No* (N) or *Don't know* (DK) against each statement.

1 The man is visiting the woman. `Y`
2 They turn on the radio.
3 There has been a train accident.
4 The train hit the back of another train.
5 It was the train driver's fault.
6 A lot of people died in the accident.
7 The accident is worse than British Rail first thought.

ORAL EXERCISES

2 Express surprise.

T: Guess what! Bob's in hospital with a broken leg.
S: *He isn't, is he?*

3 Express strong opinions.

T: Was it a good holiday?
S: *Yes, it was the best holiday I've ever had.*

1 Yes/good holiday/have
2 No/uncomfortable bed/sleep in
3 Yes/impressive building/see
4 No/bad food/eat
5 Yes/pretty hotel/stay in

4 Make negative comparisons.

T: What did you think of the food?
S: *It wasn't as good as last year.*

1 good
2 friendly
3 comfortable
4 hot
5 exciting
6 interesting

54

5 Make positive comparisons.

T: Was the food good?
S: *Yes, it was much better than last year.*
T: Were the guests friendly?
S: *Yes, they were much more friendly than last year.*

PRONUNCIATION

Diphthongs
/ɪə/ here
/eə/ there

6 Listen and circle the words you hear.

/ɪə/	/eə/
1 (here)	hair
2 we're	where
3 pier	pair
4 fear	fair
5 beer	bear

7 Listen and repeat the words and phrases.

here   there
dear   where
fear   hair

I can't hear you.
Oh dear, where are you?
Here's Clare.

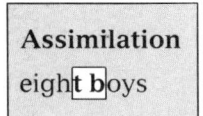

Assimilation
eigh**t b**oys

8 Listen and repeat the phrases.

eight boys   nine girls
ten men   a good book
a bad boy   a red box

STRESS AND INTONATION

Sentence stress
o O o oOo o O
It's <u>much</u> more ex<u>ci</u>ting than <u>that</u>.

9 Listen and underline the stressed syllables.

1 It's much more exciting than that.
2 A bit more impressive than ours.
3 He's much more polite than I thought.
4 It's not as exciting as yours.

Now listen and repeat the sentences.

Intonation of question tags
He's Brazilian, isn't he?

10 Listen to the conversation and repeat the question tags. Try to make your voice go down at the end of the question.

T1: Tomorrow's Monday, isn't it?
S: *Tomorrow's Monday, isn't it?*
T2: Yes, that's right. Why do you ask?
T1: I've got to go to Brighton tomorrow. You've been there, haven't you?
S: *You've been there, haven't you?*

1 Tomorrow's Monday, isn't it?
2 You've been there, haven't you?
3 It isn't far from London, is it?
4 You've got a sister in Brighton, haven't you?
5 She works in a hotel, doesn't she?
6 I'm late, aren't I?

Unit 31

READING

1 Read the article.

HARD WORK IS THE KEY TO SUCCESS

SAYS 24-YEAR-OLD

CHARLES JOHNSON

My parents came from Trinidad to make a new home in Britain. Young black people like me know no other home. I went to a local school in Leicester where most of the pupils were black or Asian. Only two pupils in fifty from that school went to university. Luckily I was one of them. When I left university, I became a journalist. Now I'm a BBC producer.

When I was young my parents told me to work hard and pass my exams. I did. However, because of that I didn't make many friends. My father used to tell me that black people had to work twice as hard as white people to be successful. I worked hard at school because I had to. Now I work hard because I enjoy it. And I've got plenty of friends too.

GRAMMAR: *used to*

2 Join the facts to make sentences about Charles, using *used to*.

1 Charles's family lived in Trinidad. — He works in London.
2 Charles went to school in Leicester. — He's a BBC producer.
3 Charles didn't have many friends. — He works hard because he enjoys it.
4 Charles worked hard because he had to. — They live in England.
5 Charles was a journalist. — He's got plenty of friends.

1 *Charles's family used to live in Trinidad but now they live in England.*
2 *Charles used to go to school in Leicester but now he works in London.*
3 *Charles didn't use to have many friends but now he's got plenty of friends.*
4 *Charles used to work hard because he had to but now he workes hard because he enjoys it.*
5 *Charles used to be a journalist but now he's a BBC producer.*

3

Clare is asking her mother, Ann, about a woman who used to live in her mother's village. Complete Clare's questions, using the verbs in the box.

| paint | live | look like | do | draw |

CLARE: ¹Where *did she use to live?*

ANN: She used to live in the old cottage at the end of the village.

CLARE: ²What *did she use to look like?*

ANN: When she was young, she used to have long dark hair and she used to wear glasses.

CLARE: ³What *did she use to do* every day?

ANN: She used to spend most of her time painting.

CLARE: ⁴What *did she use to paint?*

ANN: Country scenes mostly. But sometimes she used to draw people.

CLARE: ⁵Who *did she use to draw?*

ANN: Her friends, I think. Oh, and some of the local characters. Your grandfather, for example!

VOCABULARY: modern inventions

4

Use the pictures to complete the word puzzle. Find mystery word number 12, another modern invention.

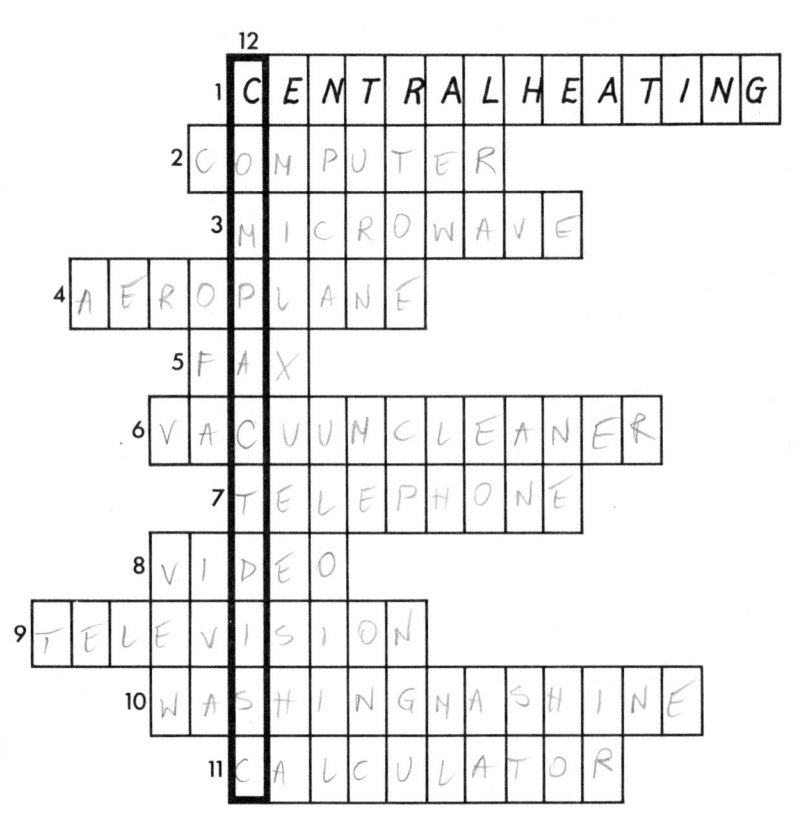

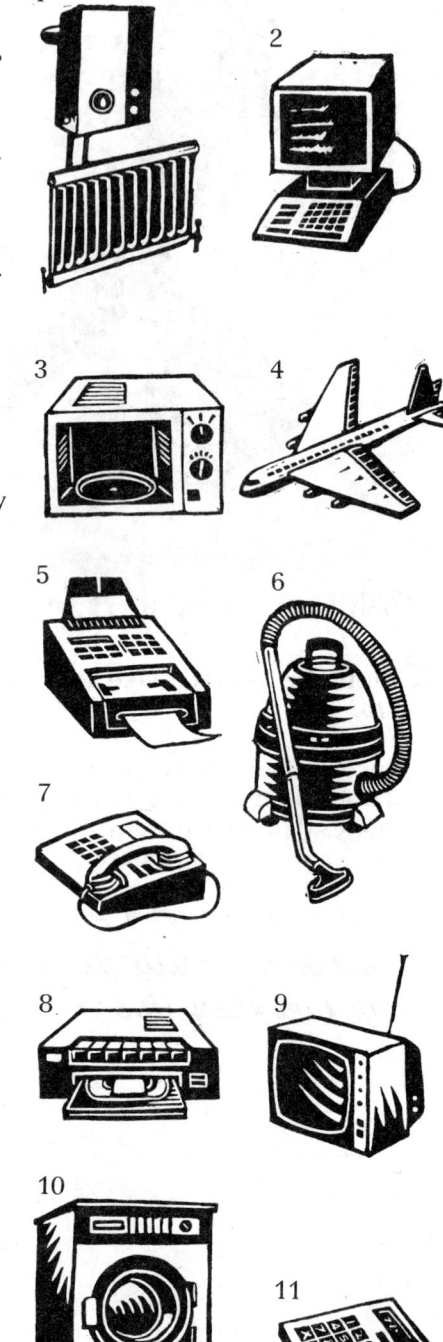

1. CENTRAL HEATING
2. COMPUTER
3. MICROWAVE
4. AEROPLANE
5. FAX
6. VACUUN CLEANER
7. TELEPHONE
8. VIDEO
9. TELEVISION
10. WASHING MASHINE
11. CALCULATOR

Unit 32

GRAMMAR: *so . . . that*

1 Use the words and phrases in the box to write a caption for each picture with *so . . . that*.

get/letter	nervous	fall/asleep immediately
see/view	tired	tear/it up
open/door	angry	break/a plate
arrive at/hotel	excited	shout/for help
go/party	frightened	take/a photo

1 *When she got the letter she was so angry that she tore it up.*

2 When they saw the view they were so excited that he took a photo.

3 When he opened the door he was so frightened that he shouted for help.

4 When he arrived at the hotel he was so tired that he fell asleep immediately.

5 When she went to the party she was so nervous that she broke a plate.

GRAMMAR: *such . . . that*

2 Last week Clare and Lisa went to a party. Bob and Jane went to the same party. Clare and Lisa liked it. Bob and Jane didn't. Use the words in the box to write Bob and Jane's opinions.

Adjective	Result
awful boring	not eat much leave early
dreadful unfriendly	nearly fall asleep talk to each other

Clare and Lisa said:

1 It was a great party!

2 They were very friendly people.

3 They gave us lovely food.

4 It was a very interesting evening.

Bob and Jane said:

It was such an awful party that we left early.

They were such unfriendly people that we talked to each other.

They gave us such dreadful food that we didn't eat much.

It was such a boring evening that we nearly fell asleep.

WRITING

3 Read the note on the right. Then, in your notebook, write similar messages for your boss and your mother saying why you did and didn't do things. Use the notes to help you.

TO YOUR BOSS
You were in a meeting which went on for a very long time and you didn't have time to finish the accounts. Then you were feeling very tired and you went home.

TO YOUR MOTHER
You got up very late and you didn't have time to do the shopping. Then it was a beautiful day and you borrowed the car to go to the beach.

Laurent,
The queue was so long that I didn't buy the tickets for the cinema. Then I'm afraid the theatre tickets were so expensive that I didn't buy them either. Sorry!
Caroline

★ ★ ★ Joke ★ ★ ★

I knew a man who was so unpopular that his phone didn't ring even when he was in the bath.

Unit 33

GRAMMAR: first conditional + future will/won't

1 Join the two parts of each sentence to make an *if* clause and use the sentences to complete the conversation between Josh and Eva.

1 you want to go — I/get some tickets.
2 we book today — we/get better seats.
3 you have to work late — I/meet you at the theatre.
4 you're very late — I/leave your ticket at the box office.
5 it finishes before 10.30 — I/take you out for a meal.
6 I go straight from work — how/you get there?
7 it's raining — I/take the underground.

JOSH: There's a Paul Simon concert next month at the Dominion theatre.
EVA: Is there?
JOSH: Yes. ¹ *If you want to go, I'll get some tickets.*
EVA: Great.
JOSH: I'll book them next week.
EVA: Why not book them now? ² *If we book today, we'll get better seats.*
JOSH: You're right. The trouble is, I sometimes have to work late.
EVA: Don't worry. ³ *If you have to work late, I'll meet you at the theatre.*
JOSH: But I might be very late.
EVA: Well, ⁴ *if you're very late, I'll leave your ticket at the box office.* What about a meal afterwards?
JOSH: ⁵ *If it finishes before 10.30, I'll take you out for a meal.*
EVA: O.K. Thanks.
JOSH: ⁶ *If I go straight from work, how will you get there?*
EVA: By bus. Or ⁷ *if it's raining, I'll take the underground.*

2 Write the verbs in brackets in the correct tense.

1 If it (not rain), we (go) to the park.
If it doesn't rain, we'll go to the park.

2 I (phone) and thank her if I (not have time) to write.
I'll phone and thank her if I don't have time to write.

3 If you (not take) your medicine, you (not get better).
If you don't take your medicine, you won't get better.

4 We (not able) to come if we (not get) a babysitter.
We'll be not able to come if we don't get a babysitter.

5 If she (not hurry), she (miss) the bus.
If she doesn't hurry, she'll miss the bus.

60

David Hill
A PSYCHOLOGIST continues our series HOW TO BE YOURSELF This week he looks at

How to get what you want

People often complain that they never seem to get what they want. The simple reason is that they don't ask for it clearly enough. If you don't make a clear request, the other person won't know what you want. If you simply sigh heavily in front of the television, how will your partner know that you want him or her to turn it off?

Another problem is that people often say 'yes' when they want to say 'no'. The trouble is that they want people to like them. They also worry too much about what others think of them. 'What will they think of me if I say no?', or 'What will she think of me if I say I don't want to go to her party?' Of course we want others to like us, but it's important to realise that the world won't come to an end if someone disapproves of us.

> **NEXT WEEK**
> How to show anger

READING

3 Read the text and answer the questions.

1 Why don't people get what they want?
They don't ask for it clearly enough.

2 What will happen if you don't make a clear request?
The other people won't know what I want.

3 Why do people 'often say "yes" when they want to say "no"'?
They want to like them.

4 What else do they worry about?
They worry about what others think of them.

5 What do people think will happen if someone disapproves of them?
They think that the world will come to an end.

4 What do you think the speaker really means in each of the sentences below? Change them into 'clear requests'.

1 Oh dear. There's a lot of washing up to do.
Could you do the washing up?

2 It's very hot in here.
Could you open the window?

3 Do you really like rock music?
Could you turn off the radio?

4 Oh dear, I haven't got my money with me.
Could you lend me some money?

5 I think I can hear the phone.
Could you get the phone?

6 A cup of tea would be nice.
Could you bring me a cup of tea.

Unit 34

GRAMMAR: past perfect

1 Last week Peter Johnson had his 30th birthday. What had he done by the time he was 30? Complete the list.

I pass my exams and get a degree.
I train as an architect.
I visit the USA.
I buy a car.
We get married.
I start my own company.

By the time he was thirty:
1 *He had passed his exams and got a degree.*
2 He had trained as an architect.
3 He had visited the USA.
4 He had bought a car.
5 They had got married.
6 He had started his own company.

2 In your notebook, write three sentences about yourself each beginning *By the time I was . . .*

GRAMMAR: past simple/past perfect

3 Write the sentences with one verb in the past simple and one verb in the past perfect.

1 She (be) very tired because she (not sleep) for two days.
She was very tired because she had not slept for two days.

2 When I (get) to the shop it (close).
When I had got to the shop it closed.

3 She (not know) him long before they (get married).
She hadn't known him long before they got married.

4 You (finish) all the questions when the examination (end)?
Had you finished all the questions when the examination ended.

5 We (arrive) late so the bus (already go).
We arrived late so the bus had already gone.

6 He (not go) to the cinema with them because he (already see) the film.
He didn't go to the cinema with them because he had already seen the film.

VOCABULARY

4 Circle the correct word for each sentence.

1 He's always late. He was even late for his own . . .
   a) church (b) wedding c) fiancée

2 I dropped my wallet on the . . . just outside the house.
   (a) ground b) floor c) carpet

3 I didn't want to wake anybody so I took off my shoes and . . . upstairs.
   a) climbed (b) crept c) ran

4 When he . . . the tree, all the apples fell down.
   a) trembled b) swayed (c) shook

5 After ten years, he had changed so much that I hardly . . . him.
   a) saw b) noticed (c) recognised

Unit 35

GRAMMAR: present passive

HOW A PLAY IS PRODUCED

| 1 Choose a play. | 2 Book a theatre. 3 Choose the actors. | 4 Design the sets and costumes. 5 Rehearse the play. | 6 Build the sets. 7 Make the costumes. | 8 Advertise the play. 9 Sell the tickets. | 10 Hold a preview of the play. |

Glossary
rehearse To practise (a play or a concert).
set The scenery and furniture for a play.
costumes The clothes actors wear in a play.

1 Use the information in the chart above to answer the questions.

1 What happens after the producer has chosen a play?
A theatre is booked and *the actors are chosen.*

2 What happens after the actors are chosen?
The sets and costumes are designed and *the play is rehearsed.*

3 What happens after rehearsals have started?
The sets are build and *the costumes are made.*

4 What happens after the play is advertised?
The tickets are sold and *a preview of the play is held.*

63

2 Complete the sentences by changing the active to the passive and adding *by* where necessary.

1 They grow tea in India, Sri Lanka and China.
   Tea is grown in India, Sri Lanka and China.

2 Police use sniffer dogs to detect drugs and explosives.
   Sniffer dogs are used to detect drugs and explosives.

3 Australians often call English people 'Poms'.
   English people are often called 'Poms' (by) Australians.

4 They do not make many films in Hollywood now.
   Not many films *are made in H. now.*

5 Scottish men often wear kilts on special occasions.
   Kilts *are often worn by Scottish men on special occasions.*

6 Over three million British people buy the *Sun* newspaper every day.
   The *Sun* newspaper *is bought every day by over three million 3. people.*

7 A restaurant bill usually includes service.
   Service *is included* in a *restaurant's bill.*

8 They usually cancel flights if there is thick fog.
   Flights *are usually cancelled if there is thick fog.*

VOCABULARY

3 Complete the definitions with a word from Unit 35 in the Students' Book beginning with *s*.

1 To look carefully for something is to *search.*

2 To find the answer (to a problem) is to *solve.*

3 To take something that does not belong to you is to *steal.*

4 To bring something into a country illegally is to *smuggle.*

5 Someone the police thinks has committed a crime is a *criminalist.*

6 A step in a process is a ....

7 The top part of something is the ....

WRITING

4 Read about the emerald, then use the notes about the diamond and the ruby to write similar paragraphs about them in your notebook.

PRECIOUS STONES
The emerald is the most brittle of the precious stones and is a rich green colour. The best emeralds are found in Colombia and are used to make jewellery. They are said to cure fever and diseases.

	Diamond	Ruby
DESCRIPTION	hardest	rarest
COLOUR	colourless	blood red
WHERE FOUND	Namibia and Australia	Burma
USE	jewellery, watches and cutting instruments	jewellery
EFFECT	makes people strong, brave and lucky in love	keeps people young and healthy

Listening and speechwork 31–35

BELLA

puts new life into your hair

BELLA CARES

LISTENING

1 Listen to four advertisements and say what they are for. Choose the best answer.

1 a) toothpaste   (b)) a hair shampoo   c) a washing powder
2 a) a radio   b) a T-shirt   c) a concert
3 a) a job agency   b) a clothes shop   c) a college
4 a) a night club   b) a coconut drink   c) a chocolate bar

ORAL EXERCISES

2 Talk about past facts.

T: Has he always driven a Volvo?
S: *No, he used to drive an old Fiat.*

1 an old Fiat
2 in Manchester
3 in advertising
4 quite long hair
5 quite slow at school

3 Talk about consequences.

You are going on a trip to Naples in Italy.
T: Are you going to go to Capri while you're there?
S: *Yes, I'll go there if the weather is good.*

1 Capri/the weather is good
2 Ennio and Rose/I have time
3 Giorgio/I have a free evening
4 the video camera/I have room in my suitcase
5 a new leather wallet/I see a nice one
6 me/the plane is late

4 Talk about past experiences.

You have been away on a long trip.
T: I expect you were tired when you got back.
S: *Yes, I was. I hadn't slept for three nights.*

1 not sleep/three nights
2 not eat/two days
3 not have anything to drink/twelve hours
4 not wash/three days
5 not see my family/six months

5 Describe processes.

T: How do they stamp all those letters?
S: *They're stamped by machine.*

1 letters/stamp
2 cows/milk
3 money/count
4 weight/check
5 sweets/pack
6 sweater/knit

PRONUNCIATION

Consonant clusters
/θr/ throw
/str/ strong

6 Listen and repeat the words and phrases.

throw	throat	strange
threw	strong	stripe
three	string	

three strong men
She threw it three times.
She wore a strange striped sweater.

Assimilation
thi s sh op

7 Listen and repeat the phrases.

this shop
these shoes
this shirt
these shops
this shape
these shorts

STRESS AND INTONATION

Sentence stress
o O o O o o O
I used to wash them by hand.

8 Listen and underline the stressed words and syllables.

1 I used to wash them by hand.
2 He used to go to my school.
3 I'd like to offer you tea.
4 I'm going to ask for a rise.

Now listen and repeat the sentences.

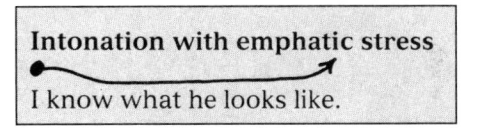

Intonation with emphatic stress
I know what he looks like.

9 Listen to the conversation and repeat the answers. A visiting professor is coming to your town and you offer to help.

T1: Does anyone know what he looks like?
T2: I know what he looks like.

1 I know what he looks like.
2 I don't mind.
3 I'm going.
4 I'll take him to lunch.
5 I can give him a lift.

Unit 36

GRAMMAR: reported statements

1 Report what your new neighbour, Emma, tells you about herself.

1. I've just left college.
2. I work in a library.
3. I'm getting married next May.
4. My fiancé is a teacher.
5. I met him at college.
6. I don't mind loud music or parties if I'm invited!

1 *She said she had just left college.*
2 She said she worked in a library.
3 She said she was getting married next May.
4 She said her fiancé was a teacher.
5 She said she had met him at college.
6 She said she didn't mind loud music or parties if she was invited.

2 A police officer has made a report about a stolen car. Use his statements below to complete the original interview.

1. He said someone had stolen his car.
2. He said the car was a Ford Sierra.
3. He said it was dark red.
4. He said he had left the car in the street outside his house.
5. He said he had left his briefcase in the car.
6. He said there was also a car radio and lots of cassettes but he couldn't remember how many.
7. He said it wasn't the first time.

OFFICER: Can I help you, sir?
MAN: Yes, you can, officer. ¹ *Someone has stolen my car.*
OFFICER: What make of car is it?
MAN: ² It is a Ford Sierra.
OFFICER: And what about the colour?
MAN: ³ It is dark red.
OFFICER: And where did you leave your car?
MAN: ⁴ I left the car in the street outside my house.
OFFICER: Did you leave anything valuable inside the car?
MAN: ⁵ I left my briefcase.
OFFICER: Is there anything else in the car?
MAN: Yes, ⁶ there is also a car radio and lots of cassettes but I can't remember how many.
OFFICER: I see. Has this happened in your street before?
MAN: Yes. ⁷ It is not the first time.

Unit 37

READING

1 Read the descriptions on the right and tick the chart to show which personality adjectives refer to which person.

	1 Sarah	2 Paul	3 Bill	4 Trish
jealous		✓		
tidy				✓
thoughtful	✓			
stubborn			✓	
generous	✓			✓
fussy				
bad-tempered		✓		

GRAMMAR: modifiers

2 Answer the questions using the correct modifier from the box.

1 How warm are these countries in August?

| not at all   quite   extremely |

Egypt *is extremely warm*.
Germany *is quite warm*.
Siberia *isn't warm at all*.

2 How dangerous are these sports?

| not very   rather   not at all |

Table tennis *isn't dangerous at all*.
Motor racing *is rather dangerous*.
Windsurfing *is not very dangerous*.

Sarah's amazing. She always remembers people's birthdays. She even remembered Mum's birthday and bought her a big bunch of flowers and some of those really expensive Belgian chocolates.

I'm fed up with Paul. Yesterday we went out for dinner and I met an old school-friend I haven't seen for years. So obviously we had a nice long chat. Paul just sat silently and got really angry. Then in the car he said he didn't want me to see my friend again!

This is typical of Bill. On Saturday we were going to visit some friends who live right out in the country. Anyway, we got lost and Bill was determined to find the place himself, so we spent an hour driving round in circles because he refused to ask someone the way!

Trish and I share a flat and we get on quite well but she's beginning to annoy me. I had some friends for dinner and washed up but didn't put the things away. In the morning she was quite angry. She said it annoyed her to see things lying around. Now she's started to organise the food cupboard. Can you believe it? Every shelf is labelled and we have to put the right things on the right shelf!

3 How fast are these ways of travelling?

| extremely   fairly   not very |

Cars *are fairly fast*.
Cycling *is not very fast*.
Aeroplanes *are extremely fast*.

4 How serious are these crimes?

| not very   quite   very |

Drug smuggling *is very serious*.
Shoplifting *is quite serious*.
Parking in the wrong place *is not very serious*.

68

Unit 38

GRAMMAR: reported questions

1 You meet a friend you haven't seen for a long time. Report the questions he asked you.

1. Where are you living now?
2. Have you finished your studies yet?
3. What sort of job have you got?
4. Have you still got your old Citroën?
5. How long do you have for your lunch break?
6. Do you want to go for a quick coffee?

Worldwide Farm Community
SEASONAL FARMWORKERS WANTED
USSR · Europe · Asia · Latin America

Over 18?
Finished full-time education?
Got a driving licence?
Speak a foreign language?
Worked abroad before?
Healthy and energetic?

IF YOU CAN ANSWER **YES** TO THESE QUESTIONS
phone 071-987 09156 and arrange an interview today!

1. *He asked me where I was living now.*
2. *He asked me if I had finished my studies yet?*
3. *He asked me what sort of job I had got.*
4. *He asked me if I still had got my old Citroën.*
5. *He asked me how long I had for my lunch break.*
6. *He asked me if I wanted to go for a quick coffee.*

2 You went for an interview for the job advertised above. Report the questions they asked you at the interview.

1. *They asked me if I was over eighteen.*
2. *They asked me if I had finished full-time education?*
3. *They asked me if I had got a driving licence.*
4. *They asked me if I spoke a foreign language.*
5. *They asked me if I had worked abroad before.*
6. *They asked me if I was healthy and energetic.*

READING

3 Read and rearrange the parts of the story, writing the letters in the correct order.

A When I got to the man's car, I put the suitcase down. He asked me where my car was parked. I replied that my car wasn't there.

B I took the suitcase back to the stationmaster. No doubt there was a very angry passenger somewhere on that train!

C I wanted to help him so I asked him if I could take one of the suitcases. He said yes, so I picked up the suitcase in front of me.

D I was visiting my relations in Yorkshire. As I was getting off a train in Wakefield, I saw that the man in front of me had some heavy suitcases.

E He looked extremely puzzled and asked me what I was going to do with my case. My case!? I said it wasn't my case. He said it wasn't his case. It was all a misunderstanding. I had picked up someone else's suitcase, thinking it was the man's.

F It was very big and heavy. The man went on ahead and I followed him, struggling with the suitcase, to the car park.

1 *D* 2 *C* 3 *F* 4 *A* 5 *E* 6 *B*

69

Unit 39

READING

1 Read the story and complete it using the adjectives in the box.

| angry   amazed   pleased   ashamed |
| delighted   worried   frightened |

'I had just completed my first year as a teacher in a London secondary school. I was very ¹ _pleased_ with myself because I thought I had discovered the perfect place for the end-of-year class picnic – on an island in the middle of the River Thames. We were able to walk across to the island on stepping stones. My students were ² _amazed_ with the place and we had a long, lazy afternoon. When we eventually decided to leave for home, imagine how ³ _delighted_ we were – and ⁴ _frightened_ – when we saw water all around us. It was high tide. I had forgotten that the Thames is a tidal river, like the sea! Six hours later we were able to walk off the island. You can imagine how ⁵ _angry_ and ⁶ _worried_ the parents were, and how ⁷ _ashamed_ I felt of the whole incident. To celebrate the end of term next year, we're having a disco in the school hall!'

2 Read the story again and answer the questions.

1 Where was the 'perfect picnic place'?
   An island in the middle of the River Thames.

2 How did the teacher and his students get there?
   They walked across to the island on stepping stones.

3 Why couldn't they get off the island?
   Because there was water all around them.

4 What was the reason for this?
   It was high tide.

5 How long did they have to wait on the island?
   They had to wait 6 hours on the island.

6 What has the teacher decided to do next year?
   He decided to have a disco in the school hall.

GRAMMAR: prepositions after adjectives

3 Complete the sentences using the cues. Supply the correct preposition each time.

1 (quite frightened)
   I don't enjoy driving on the motorway. In fact I'm *quite frightened of* it.

2 (very worried)
   Have you seen Jenny lately? I'm .... her.

3 (very proud)
   I've just painted a picture. I'm .... it. What do you think of it?

4 (very disappointed)
   You know that computer system I bought? Well, it's no good and I'm .... it.

5 (surprised)
   I didn't like the film at all. In fact I'm .... the good reviews it got.

6 (quite ashamed)
   The police arrested him outside the shop. He told them he was .... what he had done.

VOCABULARY

4 Write the correct noun for each adjective.

Adjective	Noun
1 frightened	*fear*
2 shocked	....
3 guilty	....
4 angry	....
5 disappointed	....
6 delighted	....
7 pleased	....
8 proud	....

5 Rewrite the sentences choosing a stronger adjective from the box.

| angry | hopeless | terrified | delighted |
| excellent | amazed | | |

1 She was pleased with her present.
   She was delighted with her present.

2 I'm frightened of the dark.
   ....

3 He's annoyed with her because she forgot to post his letters.
   ....

4 I was surprised at the price of petrol when I last filled my car.
   ....

5 I'm not very good at cooking, I'm afraid.
   ....

6 She used to be good at games when she was at school.
   ....

Unit 40

GRAMMAR: phrasal verbs

1 Complete the sentences to confirm what jobs you will do after your class. Choose from the phrasal verbs in the box.

| turn on | lock up | put on | take out |
| put away | turn off | | |

A: Don't forget the heating.
B: No, I'll [1] *turn it off* now.
A: Do you know where the books go?
B: Yes, I'll [2] .... in the cupboard.
A: What about the rubbish?
B: I'll [3] .... to the bins.
A: The cover has to go on the computer.
B: [4] .... now.
A: Don't leave the store cupboard unlocked.
B: No, [5] ....
A: We always leave the lights on in the car park.
B: Fine. [6] .... when I lock the main door.

WRITING

2 You work in a small gym club. In your notebook, copy and complete the notice below about evening closing routine. Use phrasal verbs to write about:

1 the floor mats and weights
2 the cash box and membership cards
3 the lights in the gym and changing rooms
4 the security alarm

Clifford Road Gym and Sports Club
NOTICE TO ALL MEMBERS

Use of the club in the evenings

Will the last person out of the club please:
• ....
• ....
• ....
• ....

Many thanks
CLUB SECRETARY

VOCABULARY

3 Complete the crossword.

(1 Across: CHAIN)

CLUES

Across

1 Men used to wear their watches on one of these. (5)
3 You use this to tidy your hair. (4)
6 Opposite of *fast*. (4)
8 Twenty dollars a week doesn't go ... (3)
9 When Jim looked ... Della's new hairstyle, he was upset. (2)
10 When Della saw her present, she was ... (8)
13 Either you go ... I go. (2)
14 When Della went out, she put ... her hair. (2)
15 To hold something or someone closely. (3)
16 Della told the hairdresser to ... off her hair. (3)
18 The remaining part. (4)
19 To sparkle with light. (5)

Down

2 Della became ... when she realised that the combs were useless. (10)
4 The hairdresser cut Della's hair ... (3)
5 A place where you can have a coffee. (3)
7 Jim's most valuable possession. (5)
11 Animals with stripes. (5)
12 Della's hair was covered in these when Jim arrived home. (5)
17 A short expression of surprise. (2)

Listening and speechwork 36–40

LISTENING

1 Lee, an athlete, is talking about his decision to join another athletic club. Listen to the conversation and circle the right answer.

1 Lee wants to leave because
   a) his present club is too expensive.
   b) it is difficult to get to his present club.
   c) the training isn't as good as at Park Hill club.

2 The trainer is not pleased because
   a) he doesn't like the other club.
   b) Lee is one of his best athletes.
   c) Lee doesn't train hard enough.

3 Lee
   a) is going to leave next week.
   b) is going to leave immediately.
   c) has decided not to leave.

2 Listen again and then complete the original conversation between Lee and his trainer.

LEE: I [1] *want to* move to a different club.

TRAINER: Which one [2] .... go to?

LEE: Park Hill.

TRAINER: Why [3] .... Park Hill?

LEE: Because [4] .... get to.

TRAINER: [5] .... with you. You [6] .... athletes.

LEE: [7] .... sorry.

TRAINER: Do [8] .... leave immediately?

LEE: Yes, [9] ....

73

ORAL EXERCISES

3 Report questions.

You went to a job interview yesterday.

T: How old are you?
S: *She asked me how old I was.*

1 how old
2 why
3 if
4 how many
5 when

4 Report statements.

T1: How old are you.
T2: I'm nineteen.
S: *She said she was nineteen.*

1 'I'm nineteen.'
2 'I like computers.'
3 'I don't mind it.'
4 'I speak French and Italian.'
5 'I'm free to start on Monday.'

5 Talk about personal qualities.

T: Is he hardworking?
S: *Yes, he's extremely hardworking. And he's quite intelligent too.*

1 hardworking/intelligent
2 serious/shy
3 jealous/moody
4 generous/thoughtful
5 artistic/imaginative

PRONUNCIATION

> **Assimilation**
> /dʒ/ would you like to
> /tʃ/ get your glass

6 Listen and repeat the phrases.

would you like to
get your glass
wait your turn
had your chance
what you want
at your service

STRESS AND INTONATION

> **Sentence stress**
> o O o o O o o O o o O
> He said that he wanted to go to the park.

7 Listen and underline the stressed words and syllables.

1 He said that he wanted to go to the park.
2 He asked if she wanted to go to the zoo.
3 I asked him to take it away from the house.
4 You must have it ready by Saturday night.

Now listen and repeat the sentences.

> **Shifting stress with the same intonation**
> I said he was NICE.
> I said he WAS nice.

8 Listen to the short conversations and repeat the answers. Make sure the stressed word changes each time.

T1: I thought you said he was horrible.
T2: I said he was NICE.
S: *I said he was NICE.*

1 I said he was NICE.
2 I said he WAS nice.
3 I said HE was nice.
4 I SAID he was nice.
5 I said he was nice.

Blueprint Quiz

How much can you remember?
Write the answers to this quiz in your notebook.

GRAMMAR

1 Which preposition is missing from the following sentence:

Someone stole her car radio . . . the night.

2 Which of the following sentences is correct?

a) *I eat meat once a week.*
b) *I eat once a week meat.*

3 Correct the following sentence:

I am here since Saturday.

4 Which of the following is NOT correct?

a) *too many people*
b) *too much salt*
c) *too many luggage*

5 Which of the following sentences is stronger?

a) *You must go to bed now.*
b) *You ought to go to bed now.*

6 Correct the following sentence:

This fish is tasting salty.

7 Put the following words in the correct order to complete the request:

later / to / back / could / him / you / call / ask / ?

8 Complete the following with tags:

a) *He works in a bank, . . . ?*
b) *You didn't enjoy the party, . . . ?*

9 What are the comparative forms of the following adjectives?

a) *clean*   b) *easy*   c) *beautiful*
d) *bad*   e) *thin*

10 Rewrite the following sentence in the passive:

They told us to be there at six.

We . . .

LANGUAGE USE

11 Agree with the following statement:

I don't like getting up early.

12 Ask the way to the bus station.

13 Offer to open the door for someone.

14 Refuse the following offer politely:

Shall I carry that for you?

15 You are choosing a sweater to buy. Ask a friend to suggest which one.

16 Give advice to a friend who drinks ten cups of coffee a day.

17 A friend is planning to go to a tropical country. Warn her/him not to forget to have an injection.

18 A friend tells you he/she has got a new job. Express surprise using a question tag.

19 Promise to send a friend a postcard from Los Angeles.

20 It is Friday evening. Say goodbye to a friend from work.

VOCABULARY

21 Which is the odd word out?

dishwasher   vacuum cleaner
laundry   microwave

22 What is the opposite of *a little*?

23 Somebody who always does what you ask them to do is r _ _ _ _ _ _ _.

24 Where should people put the ends of their cigarettes?

25 Is a *stream*:

a) a small lake?   b) a small river?
c) a small mountain?

26 What is the opposite of *sunrise*?

27 Is an *ordeal*:

   a) a part of a meal?
   b) a painful experience?
   c) a sudden incident?

28 Which of the following words has a similar meaning to the word *break*?

   hang   shatter   sink   throw

29 Which of the following words describes a person's appearance?

   selfish   shy   scruffy   stubborn

30 What phrasal verb means *to remove* (of clothing)?

CONTENT

31 What is Clare's surname?

32 Where did Lisa stay before coming to England?

33 What does Takashi Takashimi do for a living?

34 What are bagpipes?

35 Why are the crew of *Maiden* famous?

36 How did Van Gogh die?

37 What are Ayrton Senna's hobbies?

38 What is the Aboriginal name for Ayers Rock?

39 Who is Rusty?

40 What did the man and the woman sacrifice for each other in the story 'The Gift'?

Pronunciation table

Consonants		Vowels	
symbol	*key word*	*symbol*	*key word*
b	**b**ike	iː	sh**ee**p
d	**d**uty	ɪ	b**i**t
ð	**th**an	i	happ**y**
dʒ	**j**ust	e	b**e**d
f	**f**it	æ	c**a**mp
g	**g**et	ɑː	p**a**rk
h	**h**old	ɔː	s**aw**
j	**y**et	ʊ	p**u**t
k	**k**ey	uː	wh**o**
l	**l**ip	ʌ	l**u**ck
m	**m**an	ɜː	t**u**rn
n	**n**ice	ə	bett**er**
ŋ	so**ng**	eɪ	st**ay**
p	**p**ast	əʊ	h**o**me
r	**r**est	aɪ	h**igh**
s	**s**ee	aʊ	h**ow**
ʃ	**sh**all	ɔɪ	b**oy**
t	**t**aste	ɪə	h**ere**
tʃ	**ch**urch	eə	th**ere**
θ	**th**ink	ʊə	t**our**
v	**v**ase	eɪə	pl**ayer**
w	**w**in	əʊə	l**ower**
x	lo**ch**	aɪə	f**ire**
z	**z**oo	aʊə	t**owel**
ʒ	lei**s**ure	ɔɪə	r**oyal**

Addison Wesley Longman Limited
Edinburgh Gate, Harlow
Essex CM20 2JE, England
and Associated Companies throughout the world.

© Brian Abbs and Ingrid Freebairn 1991
All rights reserved; no part of this publication may be reproduced, stored in a retrieval system, or transmitted in any form or by any means, electronic, mechanical, photocopying, recording, or otherwise, without the prior written permission of the Copyright holders.

First published 1991
Seventeenth impression 1998

Set in 9.5/11pt. Linotype Versailles 55

Printed in Spain by Mateu Cromo, S.A. Pinto (Madrid)

ISBN 0 582 07535 1

Designed by Caroline Archer

Illustrated by Martin Aitchinson, Andrew Aloof, David Eaton, Ed McLachlan, Mike Mosedale, Chris Ryley, Sarah Venus

Acknowledgements
We are indebted to Random Century Group Ltd for permission to reproduce an adapted extract from *The NSPCC Book of Famous Faux Pas* by Mark Curry (pub Century 1990).

We are grateful to the following for permission to reproduce copyright material:
Ace Photo Agency for pages 1 (top) & 68 (left); Argos Distributors Ltd for page 50; Art Directors for pages 42 (top), 42 (bottom) & 68 (middle); Photo by John Birdsall for page 5; The Bridgeman Art Library/A Bigger Splash (1975) c David Hockney for page 34 (top); Camera Press for pages 26 & 65; J. Allan Cash Photolibrary for page 42 (middle); CEPHAS for pages 33 & 68 (right); Greg Evans Photo Library for pages 17 & 67; Sian Frances for page 27; Harvey Goldsmith Entertainments Ltd/Peregrine Inc. for page 60; Hutchison Library for page 52; Image Bank for pages 56 & 61; Longman Photographic Unit for pages 21, 44, 64 & 73; Photo stage for page 63; Picturepoint – London for page 22; Photo by Con Putbrace for pages 35, 38, 43 & 59; RETNA for page 34 (inset); Solo Syndication for page 53; Monica Wells for page 13.